BOLTON'S
Industrial Heritage

BILL JONES

First published in 2006 by Sutton Publishing Limited

Reprinted in 2011 by
The History Press,
The Mill, Brimscombe Port,
Stroud, Gloucestershire, GL5 2QG
www.thehistorypress.co.uk

Bill Jones has asserted the moral right to be identified as the author
of this work.

British Library Cataloguing in Publication Data
A catalogue record for this book is available from the British Library.

ISBN 978-0-7509-4442-7

Typeset in 10.5/13pt Caslon.
Typesetting and origination by
Sutton Publishing Limited.
Printed and bound in England

CONTENTS

To
Sheila, Elizabeth and John,
and Phil and Sue

Industrial archaeology, which involves the recording, research, protection, preservation and appreciation of the remains of former industries, is . . . an enormously important component of conservation policy in England. It covers the whole range of sites, buildings, structures in their landscapes, machines and processes, which illustrate industrial history. Much of this heritage survives today to hand on to future generations.

Industrial Archaeology
A Policy Statement by English Heritage
September 1995

ACKNOWLEDGEMENTS

I had help from many people during the researching and writing of this book. Firstly, I am greatly indebted to David Lewis of the Northern Mill Engine Society who offered to bring my two-fingers-and-one-thumb typescript into the twenty-first century by transferring it on to a computer and correcting some errors of fact. Denis O'Connor of Bolton Industrial History Society read through the text before publication and made some helpful suggestions. Alan Wolstenholme, the *Bolton Evening News* and Bolton Museum & Art Gallery provided many of the illustrations. I also acknowledge with thanks the authors mentioned in the Notes from whose works I culled information. The staff at Bolton Archives were as helpful as ever. And my thanks also go to the editorial staff at Sutton Publishing for help and advice. Any errors left in the text are mine. I hope that they are not too serious.

INTRODUCTION

The *Oxford English Dictionary* defines heritage as 'a nation's historic buildings, monuments, countryside, etc., especially when regarded as worthy of preservation'. There are historic monuments of Bolton's industrial past that are worthy of preservation, such as mill and factory buildings, machines, power plants, transport routes, and so on. These are of historic value because they represent some manufacturing method or technical phase or trade no longer in use today, or perhaps they are associated with an inventor or industrialist who has contributed to the country's economy and prosperity. They deserve preservation for the enlightenment and enjoyment of future generations.

Some legal protection was needed to prevent thoughtless or deliberate destruction of such monuments. Ancient monuments were first scheduled in 1882, covering earthworks, castles, and so on. In the 1960s protection was extended by listing selected buildings and structures in three grades, according to their rarity. The Town and Country Planning (Listed Buildings and Buildings in Conservation Areas) Regulations of 1990 further consolidated the situation, but (with a few exceptions) did not actually include machinery and processes.

Some noteworthy and irreplaceable historic industrial buildings and machinery of national importance have however been destroyed, as they were not legally protected. Three examples are the controversial demolition of the classic Doric portico at Euston station, London, in 1962 by the railway authorities (carried out against public protest); the deliberate scrapping of the pumping station and six steam beam engines which drained the Severn Tunnel in 1968, again carried out by the railway authorities; and the mindless fire damage caused in 1960 by trespassing schoolboys to the Britannia Bridge over the Menai Straits.

Bolton too has suffered some losses to its industrial heritage. It is regrettable that at least one of the 1828/9 stationary steam engines and rope haulage gear which operated on the Daubhill & Chequerbent Railway inclines have not been preserved *in situ*, especially as they are important to early railway history. There is some excuse for this, in that scheduling was in its infancy when rope haulage was abandoned and replaced by locomotive-hauled trains. Samuel Crompton's attic mule spinning factory and residence in King Street were demolished in 1928 and 1973, respectively. Not a single mill in the town has been preserved with engine house, engine and rope drive intact, compared with some other towns whose preserved mill engines have become visitor attractions.

In recent years public awareness of our industrial heritage has increased. On realising that much of the nation's heritage has been, or is being, lost, in 2001 the government published a report entitled *The Historic Environment – a Force for the Future*. This ensured statutory protection for all elements of the historic environment, and promised that future planning by government departments would take the historic environment into account.

Local interest in Bolton's industrial heritage was boosted by the recent television series featuring the well-known Bolton steeplejack, the late Fred Dibnah. The first series, *Step into History*, was first screened in 1999. The later *Fred Dibnah's Industrial Age* was accompanied by the eponymous book described as 'a guide to Britain's Industrial Heritage'. Although the TV series and book dealt with the whole country, there were several references to sites in Bolton, as would be expected.

Britain was once the leading industrial nation – 'the Workshop of the World', as Disraeli said in 1838 – and Bolton played its part. The town is one of the cradles of the Industrial Revolution, at least as far as textiles are concerned. The situation today is very different. Bolton and its outlying towns are no longer manufacturing centres. The staple industry was spinning high-quality fine cotton yarns and threads, for which Bolton was renowned throughout the world. Weaving and the subsequent finishing of the cloth by bleaching and dyeing were also important crafts. Some 200 spinning mills were once dotted around the town and surrounding areas, in the peak years employing thousands of men and women. Today no mill spins cotton in Bolton, Swan Lane Mills being the last to close, in 2002. Many mills have been knocked down, and of those still standing, parts are rented by small businesses. Thirteen mills have been preserved by listing, even though they show no means of how the machinery was driven.

Engineering was also an important industry in the town, with several firms manufacturing textile machinery, stationary steam engines, railway locomotives, and all kinds of capital equipment. All the big firms have gone, and thousands of skilled craftsmen have had to find alternative employment. Wrought iron and steel were once made in the town, and leather tanned, but no longer. Paper is still made in the area, but many paper mills have gone. Most bleachworks have disappeared, and coal was once mined extensively, but no longer. The last pit closed in 1960, and economically workable seams are finished. Several railway lines to surrounding towns are closed, or have disappeared. The canal which once served the town is no longer in use, and stretches of it have been filled in. Sanitary ware is no longer made in Horwich, and the former works have gone without trace.

All this makes depressing reading. The demise of some local industries is of course due to progress and changes over time. Textiles are now imported in quantity from countries where wages and overheads are low, and the machinery is more modern. Coal is not much needed today, due to the availability of other fuels such as oil and natural gas, and the reviving use of wind power. A few more modern industries have sprung up in recent years, such as the fabrication of plastics and manufacture of components for the aircraft industry. Many people now travel out of town for their employment, which was not necessary years ago when work could be found locally.

Most people have a curiosity about what their grandparents and great-grandparents did for a living, how it was done, and what social life was like. Years ago, working conditions were more harsh, often involving hard graft and long hours. There was less time available for leisure and social activities than today, and workers' housing was of a lower standard. It is only by seeing preserved buildings, machinery and houses from earlier times that a better understanding is achieved, and an appreciation of the progress made since those days becomes apparent.

Some research and recording of former days are already being carried out by local history societies, of which there are several in the town. These include industrial heritage in their programmes, but usually only in documentary form. The Manchester, Bolton and Bury Canal Society adopts a more 'hands-on' approach in its work of restoring the Bury section of the canal to make it available for water-using leisure pursuits. Another active local society is the Northern Mill Engine Society, which rescues steam engines from empty mills and restores them to working order. It is building up a collection of engines, some of Bolton manufacture, which one day will be open to the public as a steam museum.

To preserve and restore historic buildings and machinery obviously requires money. English Heritage, the statutory advisor to the government on the listing of monuments, offers financial aid to organisations it considers deserve support for their work. The Department of the Environment does the same, and the Lottery Heritage Fund awards grants to successful applicants. Local authorities sometimes give discretionary grants for the same purposes. Local societies often contribute by their own fund-raising events. A lot of restoration work is carried out by volunteers, often retired people.

Some industrial towns where there was, or still is, a dominant industry have a museum dedicated to it – for example, Kelham Island Museum for the steel industry in Sheffield, and the Black Country Museum in Dudley. Bolton, unfortunately, has no such special museum, apart from a few exhibits in its general museum, which is short of space. A plan to convert the old Moscrop Lion Oil works to a heritage centre fell through, and a more recent proposal to locate this in one of the old Atlas Mills buildings was turned down. The collection of machinery and artefacts is at present stored in a disused mill, not open to the public. Let us not forget the work of our forebears, but take pride in our industrial heritage through the monuments they have left us.

The book commences with two introductory chapters, the first on the geology of the area and the second covering the early history of the textile trade in Bolton. The following chapters each deal with a specific subject, laying emphasis on the physical remains of heritage interest which can actually be seen. Sketch maps and illustrations have been carefully chosen to accompany each chapter. Suggested further reading for most chapters can be found at the end of the book.

In general, sites lie within the limits of the metropolitan boundary (see sketch map on page 10), but occasionally a short excursion is made over the boundary if something of interest is located there, such as lead mining remains and the site of an underground waterwheel. Preserved machinery of Bolton manufacture which is outside the boundary is referred to, and its location given, so that interested readers may visit it.

It is not possible in a book of this size to cover every former industry within the area – such as silk weaving in Westhoughton and pottery manufacture in Farnworth – but it is hoped that nothing of importance has been omitted.

While this book was being researched and written, some of the historic firms mentioned disappeared. An example is Hick Hargreaves Ltd, Bolton's 170-year-old engineering company. Its site is now occupied by a Sainsbury's superstore. No doubt other firms will also disappear in the future. *Tempora mutantur*!

Bill Jones

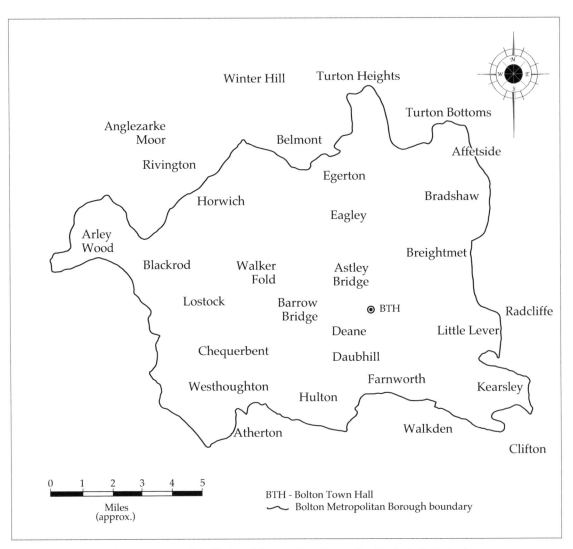

A sketch map of the Bolton Metropolitan Borough. *(Author's Collection)*

Chapter 1

Chapter 1

GEOLOGICAL NOTES

The Metropolitan Borough of Bolton lies on the north-eastern edge of the South Lancashire plain, some 12 miles north-west of Manchester. The Town Hall is 380ft above sea level, and the town is surrounded by higher ground on three sides, the south being the exception. Along its northern fringe moorland rises to a height of 1,498ft at Winter Hill, and owing to the close proximity of the moors the town was once called Bolton-le-Moors,[1] a name of Norman-French origin.

The geology of an area, the type of rocks present and the ancient movements, faulting and erosion to which they were subjected, form the framework on which the local scenery depends. They also explain the extractive industries that have developed over the years.

The geology of Bolton and its district is complex, and a general simplification must suffice here. Much of the town itself lies on deposits of boulder clay and gravel left when glacial ice melted. Below this are the Lancashire Coal Measures, overlaid in places by new red sandstone. The deeper millstone grit outcrops on the higher ground to the north around Winter Hill and Rivington Pike. These rocks and the minerals they contain have been exploited wherever they could be reached economically, though today most are worked out.

Bituminous coal has been mined in scores of places all over the town and surrounding areas. Cannel coal was mined in Westhoughton. There is documentary evidence of coal being mined from the fourteenth century onwards. Mines have been small compared with the nearby Wigan coalfield; output had peaked by the end of the nineteenth century, and no coal has been mined in the Bolton area since the 1960s. Little physical evidence now remains of this once important industry.

Fireclay, which is usually associated with coal seams, has been worked on Rivington and Smithills Moors, and it is believed that Daubhill[2] got its name from the claypits and brickworks in the area, 'daub' being an old word for clay. The manufacture of sanitary stoneware and earthenware, drainpipes and so on from locally mined clays was once a speciality in Horwich. Terracotta dug from a Little Lever coal mine was used to build the church of St Stephen and All Martyrs at Lever Bridge in the 1840s.

Abandoned sandstone quarries, from which stone was once taken for setts, kerbs and ashlar masonry, are found throughout the area. New red sandstone was used in the fourteenth and fifteenth centuries for building the older parts of Smithills Hall and Hall i' th' Wood. Today three quarries are still operating, two in Horwich and one in Harwood, providing road metal and concrete aggregate. Two abandoned millstones may be seen at Black Coppice Quarry.

Fault fractures in the surrounding gritstone at Limestone Clough on Anglezarke Moor have yielded galena (lead sulphide), barite (barium sulphate), witherite (barium carbonate) and blende (zinc sulphide). Lead was extracted intermittently from the seventeenth to the mid-nineteenth centuries from this area, known locally as Lead Mines Valley. It is believed that iron in small quantities was once smelted from ironstone nodules found in the vicinity of Smithills Hall, but if so all traces of the old bloomeries[3] are now lost. Samples of local rocks and minerals are displayed in Bolton Museum. The industrial archaeology of the extractive industries of Bolton and the surrounding area is covered in later chapters.

The high ground to the north of Bolton has some valleys left by the retreating glaciers of the last Ice Age or their melt-waters, some 8,000 to 9,000 years ago. These valleys run roughly north to south, and the streams that run in them once supplied early textile mills, bleach works and other industries sited on their banks. There are no natural lakes in the area, but several valleys have been dammed to form reservoirs for industrial purposes or public supply. The valleys have been used historically as convenient routes for reaching other towns and settlements, first by early roads and later by railways and the one canal, which follows the Croal Valley on its route to Manchester.

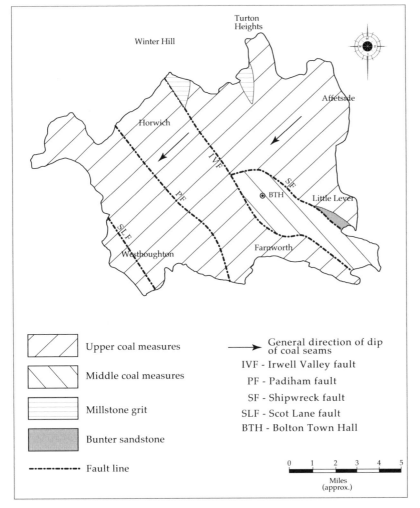

A sketch map of the solid geology of Bolton.
(Author's Collection)

Chapter 2

STONE AGE TO 1750

Artefacts found at neolithic settlements on the moors above Bolton indicate that primitive pottery was produced in the area. A stone saddle quern was discovered in 1954 near the stone circle on Cheetham Close (SD 717158), which would have been used for hand grinding wheat or barley into flour. Stone spindle whorls have been found,[1] showing that hand spinning was practised, and a Bronze Age palstave[2] was found on Charters Moss (SD 698167), indicating that metal working was possibly carried out in the area. These finds indicate the very beginnings of domestic manufacture.

Studying the transport of commodities forms an important part of industrial archaeology. The first roads in the area date from the Roman occupation. A military road, which joined Mancunium (Manchester) to Bremetennacum (Ribchester), passed through Affetside in a north-west direction. No doubt some of the local Brigantes tribesmen were press-ganged to provide much of the labour involved. Food, building materials and iron articles manufactured in the Manchester vicus (a settlement next to a Roman encampment) were probably conveyed along this route on their way to Ribchester and other Roman sites further north. Nothing of this Roman road survives above ground today, but parts of it were excavated in the 1950s[3] and again in 1975, latterly by the Bolton and District Archaeological Society. The modern successor to this is called Watling Street, after the great Dover–Wroxeter Roman road. Another less well defined Roman road runs to the west of Blackrod, from Coccium (Wigan) north towards Preston. Part of the A6 near Westhoughton is also said to lie on a Roman road.

The Danes and Norsemen arrived in the ninth century, and Bolton became subject to the Danelagh (Danelaw). There is little surviving evidence of their stay, but some place names show a Scandinavian influence. Examples are: *Anglezarke*, derived from an Old Norse name *Olafr* or *Anlaf*; *Birtenshaw*, from *birki*, meaning a birch tree; *Horrocks Scout* from *skuti* meaning an overhanging rock; and *Tonge* from *tangi* meaning a narrow strip of land.[4]

At this time yarn was spun by spindle and whorl, the spinning wheel not having been invented. Weaving was carried out on primitive vertical looms and narrow bands and braids may have been made by the Viking method of tablet weaving using woollen yarn. Primitive corn mills with horizontal water wheels, called Norse or Danish wheels, were in use in the ninth century, but there is no record of any in the Bolton area.

The Norman conquest followed the Danes and Norsemen. In 1086 the Domesday Book was compiled, and although 5,624 water mills are listed in England,[5] Lancashire was not surveyed, and so any corn mills in Bolton at that time were not recorded. The Normans left surprisingly little evidence in the area. Three place names show Norman-French origins: the name of the town itself, *Bolton-le-Moors*; *Beaumont*, which was also the name of a

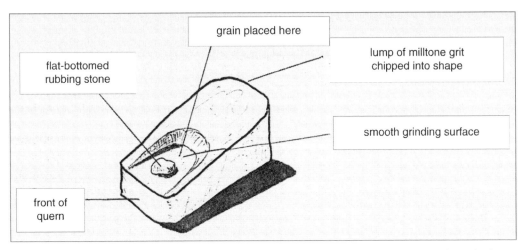

Sketch of a neolithic saddle quern. The user sits astride facing the front of the quern and grinds the grain using the hand-held rubbing stone. *(Author's Collection)*

local land-owning family; and possibly *Belmont*. The Normans did, however, introduce the manorial system all over England, under which each parcel of land or manor was a self-sufficient unit controlled by a lord of the manor.

The town of Bolton, like so many others in England, most probably grew on level ground near a river crossing, in this case the Croal, with Churchgate as the nucleus around which it expanded.[6] The surrounding land was divided into manors, each with its own lord, who owned a water-powered corn mill, since he alone had the capital to finance its construction. His peasant tenants grew their own corn and kept sheep for food and wool, spinning the wool by spindle and distaff, and weaving the yarn into cloth on their own primitive wooden looms. They had their corn ground in the lord's mill, and they fulled their woollen cloth by the laborious method of walking or treading. By the thirteenth century water-powered fulling mills were available, again owned by the lord of the manor. Later documentary evidence shows manorial corn mills still in existence in the sixteenth and seventeenth centuries on the River Tonge,[7] Bradshaw Brook[8] and Dean Brook,[9] and fulling mills on Eagley Brook,[10] Bradshaw Brook[11] and the River Tonge.[12] Other mills probably existed on other local streams.

As the population of the town and surrounding countryside gradually increased, people produced food, cloth and other commodities surplus to their own needs, and trading began. The town elders obtained a royal charter from Henry III in 1251 which permitted a weekly market in Churchgate. Two years later the Derby family granted further privileges to the town.[13]

The market cross in Churchgate records that in 1337 Flemish weavers settled in Bolton. They had been invited to England under royal protection by Edward III. He wished to encourage and expand the home textile industry and reduce dependence on imported cloth. At that time much English raw wool was exported to Flanders where it was spun, woven and dyed and returned to England as cloth. The textile skills of the incoming Flemings improved the types of cloth woven locally. One type was (confusingly, to modern ears) called cottons – a corruption of the word coatings, since it was a heavy, coarse woollen cloth used to make coats. Other fabrics introduced by the Flemings were bays, kerseys and broadcloths. In his *Itinerary* of 1540, John Leland observed that 'Bolton upon Moores Market standith most by cottons and coarse yarns. Divers villages in the moores about Bolton do make cottons.' In addition to woollen fabrics, linens were also made in Bolton. Much of the flax was grown in West Lancashire, but some came from Ireland. Wool was the principal material, and the output of woollen cloth was so great in Bolton by 1566 that an assistant alnager was appointed.[14]

It is not known when cotton was first brought into Bolton, but from about 1590 raw cotton grown in the Levant and Cyprus was being brought into England. This new material gradually began to compete with wool, and attempts were made by the influential wool merchants of the day to restrict its use by various Acts of Parliament. One example is the Act passed in 1666, which made it illegal for anyone to be buried in a shroud not made from sheep's wool. The estate of the Revd Richard Harpur of Halliwell was fined 50s because he was buried in linen in 1682.[15] In spite of much opposition, the quantity of cotton used increased year by year as demand for it rose, and also because the new industry was not controlled in the north by the southern woollen guild, with its restrictive practices. South-east Lancashire became the main cotton manufacturing centre in Britain, helped by the local climate, which aided spinning, as cotton spins better in damp conditions.

Another influx of foreign weavers occurred in 1585, when Huguenots, French and Flemish Protestants, fled their homelands to avoid religious persecution. They brought fresh textile skills to Bolton[16] and introduced the manufacture of lighter and finer materials, known as the new draperies – woollens such as serges, says and perpetuanas. It is believed they were also responsible for manufacturing fustians, a hard-wearing cloth with a linen warp and a cotton weft – a fabric which became a Bolton speciality by the seventeenth century. Dr Fuller, in his *Worthies of England*, written in 1662, says: 'Bolton is the staple place for the making of fustians, which were brought there from all parts of the country, Bolton being the principal mart for unfinished and Manchester for finished goods.' The earliest record of fustian weaving in Bolton is in the Lancashire Quarter Sessions paper for 1601, where 'George Arnould, fustian weaver of Bolton' is mentioned.[17]

The Arnould (or Arnold) family were Huguenots who came to England in the late sixteenth century. Other families of probable Flemish or Huguenot origin, and still having a local presence today are Bailey (or Bayley), Gerrard, Mercer, Molyneux (or Mullineaux), Morrell (or Morrel), Pierepoint (or Pierpoint), Russell and Seddon. The fact that the Flemish black lion is included in Bolton's coat of arms shows how much the town owes to the early influence of the Flemish weavers.

Although textiles were an important domestic-based industry in the sixteenth and seventeenth centuries, there is documentary evidence of other industries in the area, taken mainly from wills and probate inventories. Examples are tanning (Thomas Rylands of Westhoughton, 1618; James Smith of Westhoughton, 1688), rope-making (James Smith of Farnworth, 1637; George Smith of Halliwell, 1660), corn-milling (John Bradshaw of Bradshaw, 1542; Peter Unsworth of Smithills, 1587; Christopher Norris of Tonge, 1639) and nail-making (Robert Smith of Lower Hulton, 1638). Coal was being mined in Tonge in 1550, and on Winter Hill in 1587. Lead was first mined at Anglezarke at the end of the seventeenth century.

The quantity of woollen goods manufactured in and around Bolton gradually declined, and that of cotton and fustian steadily increased. By about 1700 woollen manufacture was all but dead, and cotton and fustian had replaced it. Woollen manufacture moved away to the east of the town and into Yorkshire. Bury became the geographical edge of the woollen district, as Daniel Defoe recorded in *A Tour through England and Wales*, when he visited Bolton in 1739: 'we saw nothing remarkable in this town, but that the cotton manufacture had reach'd hither' and later: 'at Bury where we observed the manufacture of cottons, which are so great at Manchester, Bolton, etc., was ended and woollen manufacture . . . began.' From an industrial archaeologist's point of view, there is almost nothing that survives from the periods so far discussed, with the exception of the building industry.

There are old halls and manor houses still standing in Bolton and the surrounding district that date from medieval times, and give examples of the building technology of that period. The principal materials of construction are stone and wood, with a limited use of wrought iron. Load-bearing walls were made from stone (red sandstone and millstone grit), quarried locally and hand-dressed by masons. Timber frames were made from local oaks felled and shaped by carpenters whose adze-marks may still be seen in some places. Mortice and tenon joints were pegged by hardwood trenails. Infilling between the main members was either by wattle and daub or by post and plaster, to form internal walls and partitions. In some cases crucks were used for the main frames, and an example of a cruck rescued from a demolished barn at Great Lever Hall may be seen on display at Smithills Hall. Other examples of crucks in situ are in the so-called 'Saxon' barns at Rivington. Roofs were covered with split stones. Smithills Hall has some sixteenth-century stained glass, but not of local origin. Three such halls of note in the area are Smithills Hall, whose oldest part dates from 1335, regarded as one of the oldest surviving manor houses in Lancashire. In 1801 the Hall became the family home of the Ainsworths, important bleachers of Halliwell. Turton Tower has a fifteenth-century stone pele tower as its nucleus, with a sixteenth-century half-timbered building attached to it. The Tower became the property of Humphrey Chetham, fustian merchant from Manchester, in 1628, and later that of James Kay, cotton spinner of Preston (d. 1857). Hall i' th' Wood, dates from 1483, where Samuel Crompton invented the mule in later years. All three buildings are now museums and Grade I listed.

By 1750 the population of Bolton was about 5,000. Cotton spinning, weaving and fustian manufacture were well established as domestic cottage industries. The invention of the flying shuttle by John Kay in 1733 speeded up the weaving of cloth, and led to a shortage of wheel-spun yarn. It took several female spinsters to keep one male weaver fully supplied with yarn.

Gilbert French, writing about Samuel Crompton, gives some idea of what Bolton was probably like in 1753:

> The market cross stood at the intersection of Churchgate, Deansgate and Bradshawgate, and to the north stretched gardens, meadows and bleaching crofts down to the River Croal, then a pleasant stream of pure water. There were warehouses and market halls in the town to hold the fustians and other piece goods made in the neighbourhood. A weekly street market was held on Mondays with merchants from London and Manchester buying the heavy fustians which were Bolton's principal manufacture. Irish merchants sold their linen yarns to Bolton manufacturers for the fustian warps. The

Hall i' th' Wood. Samuel Crompton invented the mule here in secret while renting rooms. The Hall is now a museum. *(Author's Collection)*

locally made fabrics were brought to the market on foot by the farmer-weavers. Cotton cloth was usually sold unbleached to the merchants who arranged for bleaching, dyeing and finishing to suit the market they were intended for. Several inns had large yards behind with stabling for the long strings of packhorses which the merchants used to carry their purchases. The weavers would buy more raw materials at the market and also their weekly provisions such as butter, to take home.[18]

The time was now ripe for the invention of machinery to increase the manufacturing output of cloth to match the growing demand for textiles of all kinds. Steam power was already being used to de-water Cornish mines, and the production of iron was rising. The 1750s are regarded as the beginning of that period of British history known as the Industrial Revolution. Within a few decades, spinning machines were invented – the jenny, water frame and mule, all hand-operated at first – to relieve the shortage of yarn. Some years later the power loom was perfected. Handloom weaving still continued in Bolton, however, well into the 1830s, alongside the newly created factories. After about 1840 hand weaving rapidly declined as power weaving took over.

Chapter 3

YARN MANUFACTURE

The unravelling of raw cotton, the drawing out and twisting of the fibres into a continuous length of yarn or thread for cloth manufacture, sewing cotton and the Nottingham lace trade, was Bolton's staple industry for two centuries.

In the eighteenth century yarn was made by first hand carding the tangled fibres, and then spinning them on a cottage wheel, with the spinster's fingers controlling the attenuation of the fibres and the thickness and amount of twist given to the resulting yarn. Demonstrations of hand carding and spinning on a domestic-type wheel may be seen at Quarry Bank Mill, Styal, Cheshire, and at the Helmshore Textile Museum.

In rural districts spinning was carried out in the eighteenth century by the womenfolk or a farmer who, in many cases, fitted in weaving on his hand loom with his farm work. Spinning was sometimes interrupted, as described by Henry Ainsworth, writing of eighteenth-century Birtenshaw:

> The cotton was purchased in bags or bales from Manchester dealers and was given to the weavers as raw cotton to be spun by spinsters on the distaff and spindle. At this time the spinsters who had to attend to farming operations would sometimes leave their distaff for the hayfield and thus detain the operations of the weavers causing unpleasantness between them.[1]

The adoption of the flying shuttle meant that more cloth could be woven in the same time as before, which led to a general shortage of yarn. It took up to eight spinsters to keep one weaver fully occupied, and weavers sometimes had to tour around seeking supplies of yarn in order to complete their pieces by the agreed date. This state of affairs prompted the invention of multi-spindle spinning machines, and in a period of just twenty years three different machines were invented – Hargreave's jenny in about 1765, Arkwright's water

A domestic hand-operated spinning wheel. A pair of hand cards lie on the floor in front of the spinster.
(*North West Museum of Science and Industry*)

Bolton November 20th 1780

We whose names are hereunto subscribed have agreed to give and do hereby promise to pay unto Samuel Crompton at the Hall in the wood near Bolton the several sums opposite to our names as a reward for his improvement in Spinning Several of the principal Tradesmen in Manchester Bolton &c having seen his Machine approve of it and are of opinion that it would be of the greatest utility to make it generally known to which end a contribution is desired from every well wisher of trade ———

Crompton's hand-written agreement. A list of eighty-four subscribers followed Crompton's letter with the money each promised to pay. Many reneged and Crompton only received about £60. He died a poor and embittered man. *(S. Crompton)*

Crompton's mule and creel. *(Bolton Museum & Art Gallery)*

A spinning mule team. The picture shows the spinner or minder, the side piece and little piecer. They worked barefoot on account of the heat and the slippery floor. *(Bolton Museum & Art Gallery)*

frame in 1769, and Crompton's mule in 1779. James Hargreaves (*c.* 1725–78) invented his machine in Oswaldtwistle, near Blackburn. Richard Arkwright (1732–92) lived for eight years in Churchgate, Bolton, working as a barber (a wall plaque marks the site), where he repeatedly heard of the spinning bottleneck from his customers and began thinking of how this could be overcome. Soon after leaving Bolton for Nottingham in 1768, he patented his water-frame in 1769 and a carding engine in 1775.

Samuel Crompton (1753–1827) was born in Firwood Fold, Bolton, and moved as a child to Hall i' th' Wood, where he later secretly invented the mule. He could not afford to patent it, and was persuaded to disclose its design on the promise of payment by Bolton and Manchester cotton manufacturers, many of whom later reneged on their promise once they had details of the machine, which was soon copied. The full story of Samuel Crompton is told in Gilbert French's *Life and Times of Samuel Crompton*; a reprint of the 1859 edition was issued in 1970 by Kelley. A statue of Crompton was erected in Nelson Square, Bolton, by public subscription thirty-five years after his death.[2]

Hargreaves' first jenny had eight spindles, and was intended for domestic hand use by women. It was later developed and enlarged, and by the early nineteenth-century jennies with 120 spindles were manually worked by men in small factories or jenny shops. It was because Crompton was dissatisfied with the cotton wefts he was spinning on a domestic jenny in Hall i' th' Wood that he set about devising a better machine.

Spinners' Hall, St George's Road, Bolton. *(Author's Collection)*

The mule as originally designed spun forty-eight yarns simultaneously by hand, from previously prepared rovings. It spun finer and stronger yarns than had been spun before, and enabled muslins to be woven in Bolton equal to the popular but expensive Indian imports of the day. Larger and better mules were developed, and machines of 200 spindles, partially power-driven and known as mule-jennies, were being made by the 1790s. By about 1830 fully powered self-acting mules were in use. Eventually, by the twentieth century, mules of 1,300 spindles were being built.[3] The mechanisation of spinning and weaving brought about a change in roles between men and women engaged in the industry. Spinning was now a man's job, and women took over the supervision of automatic looms.

Yarn manufacture by the American-invented ring spinning frame, which is a direct descendent of the water-frame, began to replace mules in some Bolton mills by about the 1870s. But in general Bolton mills were mule mills specialising in the finer counts.[4] By the time of the Great Exhibition of 1851 the finest yarns in commercial use were of 350 count. An extra-fine yarn of 800 count was made for display at the Exhibition at the first Delph Hill Mill, Doffcocker, a remarkable achievement for that time.[5] Today there are no mules working anywhere in Britain, apart from those which have been preserved in museums and occasionally run for demonstration purposes.

Whereas the spinster of the eighteenth century made yarn in one operation on her wheel, spinning by machine from carded cotton required several other machines at preparatory stages, each reducing the rovings step by step down to a size that can be spun. Spinning became factory-based long before weaving, and up until about the mid-nineteenth century, handloom weavers working in their own cottages were supplied with yarn from the mills. Spinners were highly unionised; the Bolton Operative Cotton Spinners' Association bought the Junior Reform Club building in St George's Road, Bolton, in 1886 as headquarters, renaming it Spinners' Hall.

Examples of historic cotton carding and spinning machines may be studied in museums around Bolton (see below). Regrettably, at the time of writing there is no textile museum in Bolton itself, but several machines are presently held in storage awaiting a decision as to where they may be displayed in public.

In store in Bolton: hand cards, spinning wheels, jenny, carding engines, roving frame, water-frame, early hand mules, late fine-spinning mule.

Hall i' th' Wood Museum, Bolton: replica of Crompton's mule.

Lewis Textile Museum, Blackburn: Hargreaves' jenny, replica of Crompton's mule.

Higher Mill Textile Museum, Helmshore: hand cards, spinning wheels, reconstructed Hargreaves jenny and later jenny, Arkwright carding engine, lantern frame, draw-frame and water-frame. Cotton waste spinning is demonstrated on 80- to 90-year-old condenser mules.

Quarry Bank Mill, Styal, Cheshire: hand cards, spinning wheels, reconstructed 16-spindle jenny, a replica of Crompton's mule made in 1912 by Dobson and Barlow apprentices. Condenser mules demonstrate cotton waste spinning.

North-West Museum of Science and Industry, Manchester: Arkwright carding engine and water-frame, jenny.

Bolton Museum: A mule made and operated by Crompton himself.

Chapter 4

HANDLOOM WEAVING

Before the introduction of factory-based steam-driven looms, weaving was a domestic industry using hand- and foot-operated wooden-framed looms, and cottage weaving persisted alongside factory weaving for several decades. Handlooms were sited in loomshops – rooms specially allocated for them and separate from the living quarters of the cottage or farm. To provide good natural light, a larger than normal window area was provided for the loomshop. Weaving was carried out by the men of the family, father and sons using yarn which in earlier days was spun on the premises by the womenfolk of the family, but after about 1780 yarn was received from the new small spinning mills. Weavers were rarely self-employed; most worked for a middleman or merchant under the putting-out system. The middleman paid for the weaving and arranged for the finishing and sale of

Town weavers' houses. The handweavers' looms were in the cellars of the houses on the left, which were sited behind the Town Hall. *(Bolton Evening News)*

the cloth. An independent weaver took his pieces to the market himself and brought fresh yarn back. A weaver usually owned the loom or looms, but the middleman often loaned healds and reeds to suit the type of cloth he wanted weaving.

One Bolton middleman was Henry Escricke (1684–1743), who was a dealer in raw cotton and linen yarn, which he bought and gave out to local spinners and weavers for conversion into cloth, either cotton or fustians. The middleman also sold cotton weft to London warehouses.[1] 'We find Escricke of Bolton making journeys to both Liverpool and Lancaster to buy cotton. In 1738 he wrote "there are about 1,000 bags at Liverpool, and Lancaster is quite full. . ." '[2]

Handloom weavers may be divided into two categories – weavers who were country-based and combined weaving with running a small farm; and town weavers, whose sole employment was weaving. The looms of farmer-weavers might be placed in an outhouse or converted barn, or in a spare room or cellar in the farmhouse itself. Town weavers usually occupied a purpose-built house or cottage, or a terrace with loomshops integral to the building.

In woollen districts loomshops were almost invariably on a top storey, but for weaving cotton the ground floor or cellars were preferred, since cotton weaves better in damp conditions. In fact, cellar loomshops often had bare earth floors for this purpose. Bolton had specialised in manufacturing all-cotton fabrics and fustians from the seventeenth century, but there are no old woollen weaving cottages with upper storey loomshops still standing today. The former weavers' cottages which do exist originally had either ground-floor or cellar loomshops. Most were built during the late eighteenth to early nineteenth centuries.[3]

Former cotton weavers' houses or cottages may usually be recognised by a row or rows of long horizontal windows which once lit the loomshop. The long windows are usually divided into separate 'lights' by stone mullions supporting long stone lintels. Three 'lights', giving a triple window, are common, but sometimes there are more. On the other hand, some loomshops were lit by normal, separate windows, and documentary evidence is usually necessary to confirm that weaving once took place in the building. Weavers' windows may be at the front or back of the building, sometimes both. Usually they were partially or completely blocked off when the building was converted into a private residence, or its use changed. The presence of long lintels is often the only evidence of former weavers' windows. Ground-floor loomshops may be in the house itself, or in an extension at the side or rear. External doors leading directly into a loomshop are rare; access was normally through the living quarters. Most cotton weavers' loomshops were in cellars, with the living quarters raised above ground level or pavement and approached up a few outside steps. This makes the loomshop really a half-cellar, with its windows partly above the ground and partly below. To admit maximum light, an open 'well' in front of the windows was usually provided.

A feature often present on some weavers' cottages is watershot masonry. Here the stone blocks forming the walls are set at a slight angle, so that the horizontal joints between them slope down outwards, to reduce penetration of the solid wall by rain and damp. This construction gives an attractive rippled surface to the walls, best seen in oblique sunlight.

Weavers' cottages may be single buildings, or arranged in terraces, and are usually two-storey buildings, excluding the cellar. In Horwich there are fifty or so early nineteenth-century weaver's cottages terraced together in Duncan Street, Nelson Street and neighbouring streets. Many are also club houses (see Chapter 15). Handloom weaving was carried on in them right up to 1861, by which time there was only one surviving weaver left.

It is estimated that there were 4,200 handloom weavers in Bolton in 1838. Most of their cottages have been demolished over the years. For example, there were once weavers' houses in Great Moor Street and behind the Town Hall. Some are still standing, and there is plenty of scope for industrial archaeologists to find and record others in the Bolton area.

The decades 1790 to 1830 were the most prosperous years for handloom weavers in Bolton, during which time they enjoyed a high social standing. But as the number of power looms increased, handloom weavers' living standards declined steadily with their earnings. In 1806 the weekly wage of a handloom weaver averaged £2, but by 1851 it had sunk to 6s 3d,[4] and those who clung to the trade were starving.

Typical domestic handlooms of the period may be seen in Quarry Bank Mill, Styal, Cheshire, and Higher Mill Textile Museum, Helmshore.

Chapter 5

Cotton Spinning Mills & Bolton Mill Architects

In the mid-eighteenth century cotton yarn was spun on manually operated jennies. The principal cloth woven was fustian, using cotton weft and linen warp, since jennies could not produce a yarn hard enough to be used for warp. Some jennies were larger than those used domestically, and several of these were housed together in a jenny shop, worked by men. There must have been many such jenny shops scattered in and around Bolton, supplying handloom weavers working in their own cottages and farms. It was not until the water frame and mule were invented in the second half of the eighteenth century that hard cotton warps became available, permitting the weaving of all-cotton fabrics.

Doffcocker, an area of Bolton which has been extensively studied by local historians, is an example of an early spinning district in Bolton. There were three small spinning mills in operation by the close of the eighteenth century, owned by Robert Lord Snr, John Heaton and Joseph Pickering.[1] These three concerns probably started up as jenny shops, and between 1797 and 1799 bought Crompton-type mules from the Bolton firm Dobson & Rothwell.[2] The mules must have been hand-operated, for there is no stream nearby that could be used to drive them. A few years later Robert Lord's two sons built a new and larger water-powered mill less than a mile away, at Barrow Bridge, using water from the Dean Brook. None of the Doffcocker mills remain today, but a picture of John Heaton's mill is in existence, taken after it had been converted into houses. A scale model of the mill as houses was made in the 1930s for Bolton Museum.[3] In the 1940s the Doffcocker area was demolished.

As the demand increased for more and more cloth, hand-worked jenny shops were superseded by water-powered machinery, and many local streams were harnessed for this purpose. Weaving, however, continued for many years as a separate domestic industry. The early water-powered mills were mostly stone built, on the banks of suitable streams on the fringes of the town, although a few were built in the town itself. Since the spinning machinery was light it could be placed on floors built one above the other to keep down the cost of buying or leasing land, although sometimes more land was acquired than was needed, with a view to future expansion. Thus the practice of multi-storey construction was started, which was followed by all future mills. The earliest recorded water-powered carding and spinning mills in the area are shown opposite:

Name of Mill	Location	Date	Stream
Langshaw's Cotton Manufactory	Eagley	c. 1783	Eagley Brook[4]
Wakefield's Mill (became Eagley Mill)	Eagley	1797	Eagley Brook
New Eagley Mill (Ashworth's)	Eagley	1802	Eagley Brook
Longworth Mill (Greenhalgh's)	Longworth Clough	before 1804	Eagley Brook
Delph Mill	Turton	c. 1782	Delph Brook
Whewell's Mill (became Lord's 2nd Mill)	Barrow Bridge	before 1793	Dean Brook[5]
Dean Mill (Lord's 3rd mill)	Barrow Bridge	1794	Dean Brook[6]
Damside Mill (Lever Bridge mill)	Lever Bridge	1784	River Tonge[7]
Thweat's Mill (became St Helena Mill)	St Helena Road	1780	River Croal
North Bridge Mill	off White Lion Brow	1782	River Croal
Horrocks' Stone Mill	Bradshaw	c. 1791	Bradshaw Brook[14]

Of the mills listed above, only parts of the original St Helena Mill and Lever Bridge Mill still stand today, and both buildings have been converted to non-textile uses.

James Watt patented the rotative beam engine, which enabled machinery to be driven, in 1779, and it was only a few years after his patent expired that steam power was applied to drive textile machinery in Bolton. The big advantages of steam were that mills could be built remote from a stream or river, and that production was unaffected by drought or frozen water. New mills were built around the beginning of the nineteenth century, with steam-driven spinning machinery, although water-powered mills continued in operation for some years afterwards, a well-known example being Egerton Mill. Some water-powered mills later changed to steam power, such as St Helena Mill. Some of the early steam powered mills include:

Name of Mill	Location	Date
Delph Hill Mill (first one)	Doffcocker	1800[9]
Peel Mill No.1	Turton Street	1797–1802
Bradshawgate (Bollings)	Bollings Yard	1787–92
King Street Factory	Back King Street	1797

Bradshawgate Mill used a steam-driven water-returning engine which pumped water from a small tank back onto a waterwheel which drove the mill machinery, the water being continually recirculated. This ensured a steadier operation of the spinning machinery than if driven directly from a rotative beam engine, as early beam engines did not maintain a constant speed.

Mills are sized according to the number of spindles they contain. The early mills were small affairs, with only a few thousand spindles. Damside Mill, for example, at the end of the eighteenth century only had some 3,000 to 4,000 spindles, and Lord's second mill about 10,000 spindles by 1816. An indication of the rise in mill size over the following years is shown by Swan Lane Mills (nos 1 & 2 combined), which had 210,000 spindles under one roof in 1905, and was at that time the largest spinning mill in the world.[10]

The first mills were designed by builders and millwrights, sometimes by the master spinner himself. The buildings were therefore strictly functional, of simple construction, using load-bearing walls mainly of stone, with wooden roof trusses and floors. Roof spans were modest to accommodate the transversely placed throstles and mule-jennies of the day. There was an ever-present risk of fire because of the combustible nature of the timber employed, and the use of candles or naked gas jets for illumination. Until the mid-nineteenth century many mills suffered from fire, some being completely burned down. Some protection against fire was obtained by plastering or cladding with sheet metal all the exposed timber surfaces, such as beams, posts and ceilings. Later mills incorporated better fire proofing: floor beams and supporting pillars were cast iron, and the floors constructed from shallow brick arches spanning between the flanges of the cast-iron beams. Several designs on this principle were developed in the nineteenth century, ranging from single-span to triple-span arches, some of which were patented. By the early twentieth century reinforced concrete floors had been introduced.

As mules were built with ever-increasing numbers of spindles, they grew longer. The width of the mills increased from around 70ft to 80ft in the mid-nineteenth century to

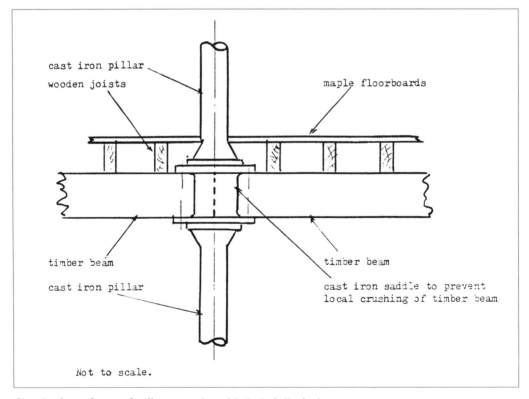

Sketch of non-fireproof mill construction. *(Author's Collection)*

St Helena Mill, 1780, Bolton's oldest. This is the remaining part of the mill and is still extant. It is now occupied by the Probation Service. *(Author's Collection)*

150ft by the first decade of the twentieth. Falcon Mill in Handel Street, Halliwell, built in 1907, is an early mill built with reinforced concrete joists and floors, designed by the Bolton architect George Temperley (1851–1927).

By the mid-nineteenth century brick-built mills were being erected with steel frames to carry the floor loading, the walls merely forming an external enclosure and carrying practically no load. This permitted larger windows to be used to give better interior light to the wide buildings. Where concrete floors were used, large square-headed windows were usually employed, although arched windows were sometimes used for decorative effect. Mills were by then being designed by architects in consultation with engineers, so a certain amount of decoration and embellishment was built into mills to improve their external appearance.

The positioning of machinery was very similar in most mills. Cotton preparation was usually carried out on the ground floor, where the bale openers and carding engines were sited. Sometimes the ground floor was wider than the floors above, to provide sufficient space for all the preparation machinery needed. Spinning machinery was placed on the floors above, with access stairways to each floor. In some mills the stairways were internal, in others the stairs were enclosed in an external tower against one outside wall. Some mills had cellars for conditioning the yarn. Another external feature often present in early mills is a latrine tower containing privies or lavatories for each floor.[11]

As firms prospered, additional mills to increase the number of spindles were built on adjacent land. The first mill would then be called No. 1, and subsequent mills numbered consecutively. Some firms built up large complexes, an example being the Atlas mills of

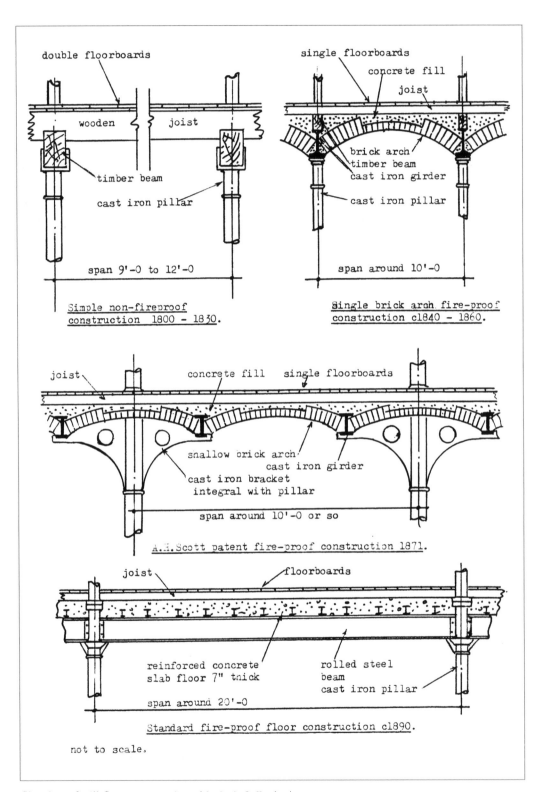

Sketches of mill floor construction. *(Author's Collection)*

James Musgrave & Co. on Chorley Old Road/Mornington Road, where six separate mills were built between 1864 and 1888 on the same site. Mills 1 to 4 were demolished in 1992, and the site is now occupied by Morrison's supermarket, although some buildings of the original complex still stand, including Atlas House, the original mill offices, and No. 4 Cotton Store, now the Museum of the Northern Mill Engine Society. Mills 6 and 7 still stand across Mornington Road, together with No. 8 in Shipton Street (Mill No. 5, on a separate site in Marsh Fold Lane, was demolished in the 1980s). Mills built after the first one naturally took advantage of later developments and improvements in machinery and building construction. Some mills were built as double mills, which meant that two mills of similar size were built end to end, with a central engine house to serve both. The two mills may have been built at the same time, but there are examples where No. 1 mill and an oversize engine house were built first, and No. 2 mill added at a later date, with a second engine in the space reserved for it. Swan Lane mills are such an example, with No. 1 built in 1902 and No. 2 added in 1905.

The introduction of steam power generally brought about new features to the external appearance of mills, such as a boiler house, engine house, chimney and a large lodge for cooling water for the condenser, although some engines were installed inside the main building. The earliest engines were beam engines working at low steam pressures and needing a tall engine house to accommodate them. Steam was provided at first by simple boilers, such as the wagon top boiler, and later by the Cornish boiler. After the late 1840s the Lancashire boiler rapidly became the most common source of steam in textile mills, with several boilers arranged side by side in a bank to generate enough steam for the large engines

Astley Bridge Mill, 1926, Bolton's newest. *(Bolton Museum & Art Gallery)*

installed. External engine houses were usually given extra architectural embellishment, to emphasise the importance of the power source.

Horizontal steam engines were introduced in the 1860s – single-cylinder ones at first, developing over the years to large compounded multi-cylinder units. Horizontal mill engines needed more floor space than verticals, so their houses were larger but with a lower roof. Regrettably, no engines have been preserved *in situ* in Bolton mills, as they have in several surrounding textile towns. However, a selection of engines of different types can be seen in the Northern Mill Engine Society's museum in Mornington Road on the Morrison's supermarket site, though only one is of Bolton manufacture.

Power from a waterwheel or steam engine was distributed to the spinning machinery via lineshafting on each floor of the mill. The earliest method was via a vertical shaft at the waterwheel or engine end of the mill, which rose up through each floor in turn. The prime mover drove the shaft via bevel gears. More bevel gears on the vertical shaft drove the line shaft on each individual floor. The final drive to each mule was by flat leather belt and iron pulleys. After the late 1870s new mills adopted rope drive. This comprised several cotton ropes running in V-shaped grooves cut in the rim of the engine flywheel, driving similar but smaller grooved pulleys on the separate lineshafts, the final drives being flat leather belts as before. The main driving ropes ran upwards in a vertical space known as the rope race, which connected each floor to the engine house. The first Bolton mill with rope driving was Mount Pleasant Mill, Bury Street, in 1876.

Lineshafting was positioned high above the machinery and ran the full length of the building, supported in bearings attached to the cast iron pillars, which supported the floor above. Arrangements to hold the bearings were either cast into the pillars, or collars were provided on the pillars to support clamped-on bearing brackets.

When electric power became available in the early twentieth century steam engines were gradually dispensed with. At first large electric motors were installed, one on each lineshaft; later each machine was fitted with its own smaller motor to give individual drives, and the lineshafting was removed. The first all-electric mill dispensing with steam-raising plant and taking all its power from the public electricity supply was Astley Bridge Mill in Blackburn Road, built for Sir John Holden between 1920 and 1926. A scale model of this building is in Bolton Museum; the mill was occupied until recently by Littlewoods' mail order company. Some mills, such as Falcon (1904–8), generated their own electricity on site from a boiler plant supplying steam to drive a turbine coupled to a generator.

Many mills have an ornamental tower, which often displays the name of the mill. Usually the tower is an extension of a staircase tower, and hidden in the top is a large water tank which supplies the sprinkler system. Sprinklers were invented in the USA in about 1880 for automatic fire extinguishing, and were quickly adopted by textile mills in Britain. The flat roofs of some mills also served as a water reservoir for the same purpose.

Competition from cheaper fabrics produced overseas gradually brought about a decline in British cotton manufacture, at first in the export market and later in the home market. In the years immediately following the First World War, cotton production in Britain reached its pinnacle. In 1919 Bolton had 120 spinning mills in operation, with 9.5 million mule spindles and 2 million of the newer ring spindles, mostly turning out the fine counts for which the town was renowned.[12] As the years went by mills began to close, and by about 1967 there were fewer than forty mills still spinning cotton in the town. Many others had been changed to alternative uses, and others had been demolished or lay empty. By January 2001 only one mill was still producing cotton, Swan Lane No. 1 Mill. The sites of demolished mills have been redeveloped, mainly for housing, retail or commercial use, some for car parks. Many of the features described above may still be observed from the outside, and much of the internal structure can still be studied in those old mills which are now DIY or furniture stores, where public access is possible.

Mules were not made fully self-acting under power until about the 1830s. The American-invented ring spinning machines, which spun by a continuous action rather than the intermittent action of the mules, were adopted in Bolton after about 1870 by the more progressive firms. Although in later years modernisation took place in some mills, Bolton mills remained predominately mule mills, with many of the mules made by the local firms Richard Threlfall and Dobson & Barlow. Even Astley Bridge Mill, Bolton's newest mill of 1926, was equipped with four times as many mule spindles as ring spindles.

Some firms extended their operations to include cloth manufacture as well as spinning yarn, resulting in integrated mills which had a single-storey weaving shed attached to the multi-storey spinning mill. (Weaving by power looms forms the subject of the following chapter.)

Although no engines have been preserved *in situ*, thirteen mills in Bolton and district have legal protection against demolition or major alteration by being listed under the Town and Country Planning Regulations 1990. They are:

Name of Mill	Date	Function	Location	Grade
Astley Bridge Mill	1926	S	Hill Cot Road, Astley Bridge	II
Beehive Mills Nos 1 & 2	1895, 1902	S	Crescent Road, Great Lever	II
Cobden Mill	c. 1890	S	Gower Street, Farnworth	II
Croal Mill	1908	S	Blackshaw Lane, Deane	II
Eagley Mills Nos 2 & 3	c. 1910	S&W	Hough Lane, Eagley	II
Falcon Mill	1907	S	Handel Street, Halliwell	II
Gilnow Mill	1868	S&W	Gilnow Road, Gilnow	II
Grecian Mills	1845	S	Lever Street, Great Lever	II
Horrockses Mill	1883	S&W	Lorne Street, Farnworth	II
Kearsley Mill	c. 1906	S	Crompton Road, Prestolee	II
St Helena Mill	1780	S	St Helena Road, Bolton	II*
Swan Lane Mills 1 & 2	1903, 1906	S	Higher Swan Lane, Daubhill	II*
Swan Lane Mill No. 3	1914	S	Higher Swan Lane, Daubhill	II*

S = spinning, W = weaving, 2* = an important example in Grade II

The early water-powered mills of the late eighteenth century were situated mainly on the streams north of the town. The nineteenth-century steam-powered mills began to be built out of town on cheap land, and were gradually surrounded by streets of terraced houses as the town expanded. No mills appear to have been built alongside the Manchester, Bolton

& Bury Canal, unlike those built in neighbouring textile towns that have canals. As the industry declined, mills either disappeared or were changed to other uses, but 138 mills remained in the borough[13] in 1997, giving plenty of scope for industrial archaeologists to study the remains of what was once an important industry in Bolton and its surrounding districts.

Statistics showing how the textile industry had declined in Bolton have been published. In 1911, 15,076 men and 21,008 women were employed in the borough, and by the 1980s the totals had fallen to 880 men and 1,730 women. In 1929 there were 216 spinning mills and twenty-six bleachworks or dyeworks.[14] Today no cotton mills and only two dyeworks (Belmont Dyeing and the Ainsworth Finishing Company on Bury New Road) remain in production.

BOLTON MILL ARCHITECTS

Several local cotton mills were designed by professional architects, and some notes on their principal practices follow.

Early mills were designed and constructed by the combined efforts of engineers, builders, millwrights, carpenters and the prospective owner. The buildings were of simple design, with little thought given to providing an attractive appearance. Professional architects of the day were engaged in designing and supervising the construction of churches, gentlemen's houses, the mansions of the landed gentry, important public buildings and so on. Industrial architecture only really began to take off in the mid-nineteenth-century, when the increasing numbers of cotton and woollen mills encouraged some architects to concentrate on that type of work.

The large cotton spinning towns of Bolton and Oldham provided scope for mill architects. Oldham in particular had several important architectural practices specialising in this class of work, such as the Stott family. Some notable mills were built in Bolton, such as Swan Lane, designed by Stott & Sons. Bolton also had some well-known architects who were responsible for many local mills, and others built elsewhere. The three most important were George T. Woodhouse, the firm of Bradshaw, Gass & Hope, and George Temperley & Son.

In 1853 George T. Woodhouse (1827–83) had an office in what is now the Georgian conservation area of Silverwell, off Bradshawgate, and later in 1861 in St George's Road. From 1860 to 1872 he was in partnership with Edward Potts (1839–1909) of Oldham. During this period they designed some mills in Oldham. At one time he was also in partnership with W.J. Morley of Bradford. Woodhouse was responsible for Sunny-side Mill, Daubhill (1872–4), built for Tootall, Broadhurst, Lee, and Peel No. 3 Mill, Turton Street (1876), built for George Knowles & Sons. (This mill was known locally as 'The Glass House', because of the extensive use of large glass windows, unusual for the time.) These are just two examples of his Bolton mills; there are many more. He also designed several mills outside Bolton, among which are Gidlow Mills, Wigan (1865) for Ryland & Sons; Bliss Mill, Chipping Norton, Oxfordshire; and Victoria Mill, Miles Platting (*c.* 1869) for W. Holland & Sons. Among his non-mill, non-industrial work he was joint architect with William Hill of Leeds for Bolton Town Hall from 1866 to 1873.

A painting of Dean Mill, Barrow Bridge, *c.* 1800. The mill has a plain stone-built exterior, designed by its owners, the Lord brothers. *(Author's Collection)*

Gilnow Mill, Bolton, was built in the Italianate style in the 1870s. *(Author's Collection)*

Bradshaw, Gass & Hope, 19 Silverwell Street, was founded in 1862 by Jonas James Bradshaw (1837–1912), in premises it still occupies today. In 1880 a nephew, John Bradshaw Gass (1855–1939), became a partner, and the name changed to Bradshaw & Gass. In 1902 Arthur John Hope (1875–1960) became a partner and later, in 1913, the firm changed its name to Bradshaw, Gass & Hope, the one it still bears today. The practice was further extended in 1920 by two more partners, William Scott (1882–1956) and James Robertson Adamson (1883–1943). During the firm's long history they designed many Bolton mills, including Eagley No. 2 Mill (1893) for Chadwick; Croal Mill, Callis Road (1907–8) for the Croal Spinning Co.; Mossfield Mill (1914–16) for John Knowles; Egyptian Mill (1919–23) for the same firm, and Astley Bridge Mill (1920–6) for Sir John Holden. Mills outside Bolton include Howe Bridge Mills Nos 1, 2, 3 and 4 (1875–1900), Atherton; Leigh Spinners Mills (1913–15) and many more. Their non-industrial work includes Miners' Hall (1914), at the corner of Bridgeman Place and River Street; Westhoughton Town Hall (1903); Spinners' Hall (1880), St George's Road; Le Mans Crescent (1937); various churches, schools, mill owners' houses; and thirteen cottages in Port Sunlight (1906–8). The fact that the firm diversified into other work when mill building ceased explains why Bradshaw, Gass & Hope are still in existence today.[15]

The firm of George Temperley & Son was founded in 1880 in Bradford Buildings, Mawdesley Street, Bolton. In 1927 it moved to 122 St George's Road, and stayed there until 1960. George (1851–1927) had served his articles under George Woodhouse, during which time he had been involved in the design of Bolton Town Hall. (George's son was Thomas (1875–1960). The firm designed Falcon Mill, Handel Street (1907) and more than twenty other major mills. It also designed the first cotton-spinning mill in Japan.[16] An important non-mill undertaking was the design of Spa Road electricity generating station for Bolton borough (1894). When the textile industry declined the firm turned to domestic and commercial work.

Other architects' firms in Bolton include Cunliffe & Pilling, which built Lostock Junction No. 2 Mill (1900) for William Heaton.[17] Ormrod, Pomeroy & Foy designed Victoria Mill, Chorley New Road, Horwich (*c.* 1904) for the Taylor family.[18] Potts, Son & Hennings of Manchester and Oldham had an office in Bolton (Potts was partner to George Woodhouse from 1860 to 1872). Thomas Haselden, another Bolton architect, designed Eagley No. 1 Mill (1883) for Chadwicks.[19]

Professional architects contributed to improvements in mill construction and safety by adopting fireproof designs, where combustible materials such as wood were eliminated. Timber pillars supporting floors were replaced by cast iron. Wooden floors were in many cases replaced by solid floors supported on shallow brick arches spanning between cast-iron beams. Concrete floors and concrete beams and joists were first introduced at Falcon Mill in 1907, by George and Thomas Temperley. Patents for non-combustible floors were taken out by Stotts of Oldham.

Architects also improved the external appearance of mills, introducing styling such as the Italianate 'palazzo' look, the French 'hotel-de-ville' or the Palladian style, which replaced the stark, plain appearance of early mills. This is well illustrated by comparing a painting of Dean Mill, built in about 1800, with a photograph of Gilnow Mill, built in the 1870s (see page 35). Some mills were decorated by coloured bricks or horizontal banding in yellow terracotta, to contrast with the monotonous red brick walls. Projecting piers or buttresses

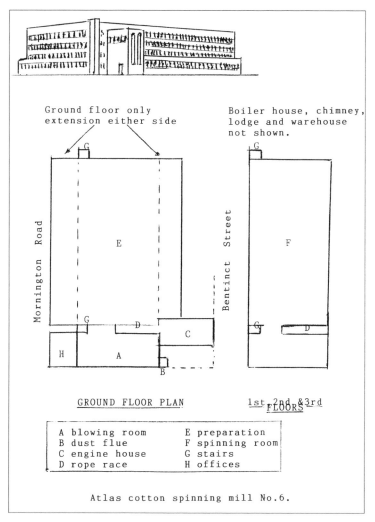

Left: Sketch plan of Atlas No. 6 Mill. The mill was built in 1888 and closed in 1964. It had 84,000 mule spindles driven by a 2,500hp Musgrave engine. The building is now in multi-occupancy. *(Author's Collection)*

Right: Automotive Products' chimney being demolished. At one time there were nearly 200 chimneys in Bolton, each churning out smoke and soot. Automotive Products Ltd was formerly North End No. 2 Mill in Tippings Road. *(Bolton Evening News)*

running up between windows or on blank walls are other external features used to add interest to a mill's appearance. Offices, main entrance doors and especially engine houses were given extra attention to emphasise their importance. Often the top of the tall chimney was decorated with a fancy oversailer, and the name of the mill was picked out high on its side to advertise its presence among the rows of terraced houses which surrounded it. Decoration and architectural embellishment added to the building cost of a mill. But the hard-headed Lancashire businessmen of the day were well aware that a good-looking, impressive building raised the confidence of visiting yarn buyers, and were quite happy to meet the extra expense.

Chapter 6

WEAVING BY POWER LOOM

Cloth manufacture on power looms began in the 1820s and '30s in Bolton, and some cotton spinning firms extended their scope by adding weaving to their operations. Weaving by hand still continued for several years, but gradually weavers left their cottages for the factory. Those handloom weavers who carried on concentrated on specialised and fancy weaving, since they could not compete against the straightforward cloth produced in quantity by steam-driven looms.

It was soon discovered that weaving by power was best done in a single-storey building, or shed, as it is called. The heavy looms and the vibration they make require strong and expensive floors, and the good light needed by weavers to detect and correct any imperfections in the cloth was best obtained in a single-storey building lit naturally from overhead. Weaving sheds adopted the north light or saw-tooth roof. This comprises a roof formed by a number of ridges with sloping sides of unequal length running across the shed, and supported on rows of cast iron pillars. The steeper, shorter slope is glazed, with the other longer slope solid. The glazed slopes face north, or as near north as the site permits, since this direction gives the best overhead natural daylight illumination without glare from

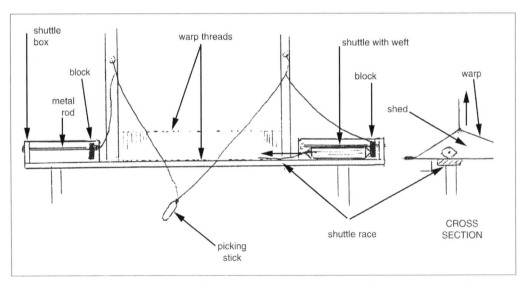

A sketch of John Kay's flying shuttle. The flying shuttle speeded up handloom weaving by allowing the weaver to jerk the picking stick to send the shuttle carrying the weft rapidly from side to side. *(Author's Collection)*

Weaving shed, Sunnyside Mill. *(Bolton Museum & Art Gallery)*

the sun. Very little development in the design of weaving sheds took place over the years, except the substitution of steel for timber in the roof construction. Weaving sheds tend to be strictly functional in appearance. Looms were arranged in rows facing each other, so that the weaver attending to them only had to turn round to face each row of machines. Weaving became a female job, with each woman looking after several looms.

When a weaving shed was added to a spinning mill, an extra steam engine was usually installed to drive the looms. Power was transmitted from the engine either by shafts and bevel gearing to overhead lineshafting, or by grooved pulleys and ropes to the overhead lineshafting. The final drive to each loom was by flat leather belts and pulleys. The rope drives were usually contained in a narrow passageway called the rope alley, running across the width of the shed and separated from the looms by a wall.

In an integrated mill, where the weaving shed and spinning mill were built at the same time, one large steam engine would normally be used to drive both departments. In some installations the weaving shed was driven by a long horizontal shaft from the main engine. As with spinning mills, electric drives eventually superseded lineshafting, and the engine and forest of belt drives (often the cause of accidents) were eliminated. In addition to the looms, a weaving shed had space for storing yarn, reeds and healds, and an area for a bobbin creel used when building up the warp beams.

A Northrop automatic loom. *(Author's Collection)*

Although Bolton was principally a spinning town, by 1919 there were some seventy firms weaving cloth, with a combined total of 40,000 looms.[1] A particular speciality of Bolton weavers was woven coverlets or cotton quilts. Today there is little cloth produced in the area; the north-east Lancashire towns are now the main centre of cloth manufacture. Three integrated mills in the Bolton district with attached weaving sheds are protected by listing: Eagley Mills Nos 2 & 3, Hough Lane, Eagley; Gilnow Mill, Gilnow Lane, Bolton; and Horrockses Mill, Lorna Street, Farnworth. All are listed Grade II.

Chapter 7

BLEACHING, DYEING & FINISHING

Before a cotton fabric can take a dye or a coloured pattern, or be sold white, it has to be bleached to remove its natural off-white colour and any impurities it might contain after leaving the loom. This whitening is done by an oxidation process. Before the onset of the Industrial Revolution, and up to about the beginning of the nineteenth century, bleaching was carried out by exposing the cloth to the action of sunlight for long periods, a process known as grassing or crofting. The pieces of cloth were pegged out on grass in a bleach croft and regularly turned over and washed. The whitening action was hastened by scouring the cloth in an alkaline lye made from the burnt ashes of

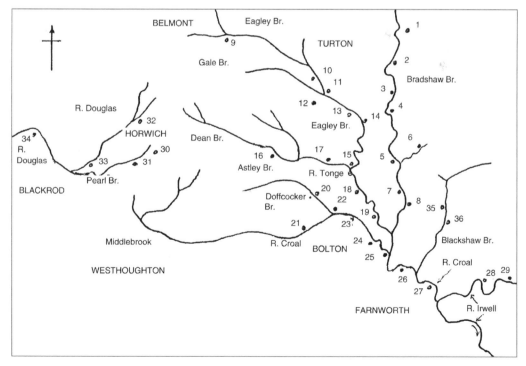

A sketch map of the sites of Bolton bleachworks. The numbers correspond with the list of bleachworks and crofts on pages 44–6. *(Author's Collection)*

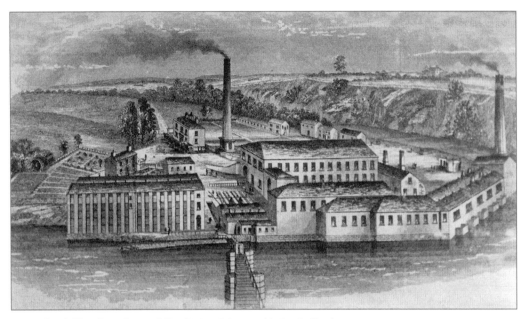

Lever Bank Bleachworks, *c.* 1850. *(Bolton Museum & Art Gallery)*

certain plants – a process called bowking – and then treating the cloth with a dilute acid to neutralise it. Sour buttermilk was used originally, followed later by dilute sulphuric acid produced by the lead chamber process.

Bolton became an important cotton-bleaching centre, with a large number of bleaching firms using water from local streams. Many bleach crofts lay to the north and north-west of the town centre, where the streams of soft, pure water ran off the higher moorland. The sketch map (p. 41) shows the sites of the principal bleachers. All the earliest firms had large bleach crofts adjacent to their works and close to a stream for easy access to water.

The pieces of cloth pegged out day and night were temptations to thieves, and bleach crofts were guarded by night watchmen, and often by hidden mantraps and spring guns. A mantrap and blunderbuss of the type used for this purpose can be seen in Turton Tower Museum. Nevertheless, the stealing of cloth, known as croftbreaking, did occur even though it was a capital offence, and newspapers report men being executed or transported for the offence.[1]

Bleaching by sunlight was a very slow labour-intensive process. It could only be carried out in the summer months, and so bleachers looked for faster alternatives. By about 1790 chemical bleaching was introduced to Bolton, mainly with the help of two Frenchmen, Mathieu Vallet (1732–1823) and a Monsieur Tenant, who worked with the Ainsworths at Halliwell Bleachworks perfecting the method. Development work on chemical bleaching was also carried out at Wallsuches Bleachworks around the same time. Cloth was bleached white with chlorine, which reduced the time required from the months needed by the atmospheric method down to a few days. The process could also be carried out all year round, and under cover. The old bleach crofts were generally disposed of, and the land which was released was given over to other uses. For example, the original bleach croft of Halliwell Bleachworks is today part of Moss Bank Park. Some firms, however, carried on with atmospheric bleaching, possibly using it in addition to chemical bleaching. A painting dated 1837 shows Slater's bleach croft still in use at their Dunscar Works.[2]

Closely associated with bleaching is the dyeing and printing of cloth, and other processes such as gas singeing, calendering and (after 1850) mercerising. All these processes were often carried out on the same premises, the firm finishing off the cloth to the specification of the merchant on a commission basis. Before roller printing was developed, patterns were printed onto cloth using wooden hand-blocks engraved with the design. Examples of hand-blocks and information about the early dyes used can be seen at Quarry Bank Mill, Styal.

Bleachworks are generally made up from a number of separate buildings grouped together, built from brick or stone with wooden roof-trusses. Mostly single-storey, they are usually purely functional, with little or no architectural decoration. Each building is devoted to a particular purpose, indicated by its name. There is a grey room for cloth awaiting bleaching, a boiling or bowking house, washing machines, a dye house if dyeing is undertaken, heated drying sheds, and so on. The primitive machines in early bleachworks were water-powered; later on, small steam engines were installed in those departments needing power. Coal-fired boilers also provided the process hot water for kiers, and so on. The bleaching room was still called the croft, even when it was used to carry out chemical bleaching indoors. The works might also have its own gas-making plant for lighting and gas singeing, if this was part of the service offered.

Wallsuches Bleachworks, built in 1777. Bleaching ceased in 1933. The factory bell is shown here. *(Author's Collection)*

Paper-making works are very similar to bleachworks in the type of buildings used, and the same need for large quantities of water. There are instances where sites have changed use from paper-making to bleaching, and vice versa, during their history. Crompton's Farnworth Paper Mill is an example. It closed in 1883, and lay empty until in 1894 when it reopened as Champion's Bleachworks.

Many bleachworks had closed by the 1960s. Some were demolished and the sites redeveloped; others occupied by a range of small businesses. Only two of those listed are still operating: Belmont Bleaching and Dyeing and the Ainsworth Finishing Co. Two former bleachworks are listed (Grade II) by English Heritage: Wallsuches Bleachworks (Horwich) and the remaining parts of Halliwell Bleachworks, including the well-known Barrow Bridge chimney, which in spite of its name has nothing to do with Barrow Bridge village; it served the bleachworks, exhausting smoke and fumes high into the atmosphere. Wallsuches is empty at present, though applications have been made to develop it for residential use.

Of other bleachworks, the principal remains are often the reservoirs (where they have not been filled in). The foundations of the buildings of Horrobin Works are visible if the water level of Jumbles Reservoir falls low enough in the summer months. Some of the remaining buildings of the nearby Bradshaw Works have been converted into flats, and the chimney of the former Quarlton Vale Bleachworks stands isolated in a field; the site of the bleachworks itself is now a housing estate. Substantial buildings still survive at Dunscar, Little Bolton, Undershore and Breightmet Bleachworks. Belmont Bleachworks and the Ainsworth Finishing Co. continue in production, in largely nineteenth-century buildings.

Mathieu Vallet's son Victor went into partnership with Richard Ainsworth of Halliwell Bleachworks in the 1790s to form a company making dyes. They built a small dyeworks close to the Doffcocker Brook, in what is now called Valletts Lane, Bolton, but went bankrupt in 1801. The building was then converted into a row of cottages for handloom weavers, which still survive today as private residences.[3]

BOLTON AND DISTRICT BLEACHERS

	Title	Date	Location	Map ref. (all SD)	Name of Firm
	Bradshaw Brook				
1	Quarlton Vale Print & Bleachworks	1825	Turton Bottoms	7406 1583	Spencer, Smith & Fairclough
2	Black Rock Bleachworks	1890	Turton Bottoms	738 158	James Hardcastle
3	Horrobin Works	1834	Jumbles, Bolton	7334 1458	J. Ainsworth, then F. Cort
4	Bradshaw Works	1782/5	Bradshaw Lane, Bolton	7315 1288	James Hardcastle
5	Firwood Bleachworks	1803	off Thicketford Road	7336 1100	Thomas Hardcastle
6	Harwood Vale Bleachworks	1865	Longsight Lane, Bolton	7394 1147	Nathan Ramsden
7	Undershore Bleachworks	1884	Crompton Way, Bolton	7358 0974	Knowles & Green
8	Toothill Bleachworks	*c.* 1784	Crompton Way, Bolton	7367 0954	James & Whitehead

Title	Date	Location	Map ref. (all SD)	Name of Firm
Eagley Brook				
9 Belmont Bleach & Dyeworks	before 1823	Egerton Road, Belmont	6774 1571	Belmont Bleach & Dye
10 Egerton Dyeworks	1829	off Blackburn Road	7052 1452	Derbyshire, Smith & Taylor, then Deakins
11 Dunscar Bleachworks	1750	Blackburn Road, Dunscar	7117 1344	Slaters
12 Springfield Bleachworks	1836	Springfield Road, Bolton	7080 1320	Longworths
13 Eagley Mills Bleachworks	c. 1820	Eagley Way, Bolton	7167 1313	James Chadwick
14 Eagley Bleachworks	1887	Paper Mill Road, Bolton	721 1296	Taylor & Nicholson
15 Waters Meeting Bleachworks	1852/3	Tippinge's Road (now Waters Meeting Road)	7200 1113	Eden & Thwaites
Dean Brook				
16 Halliwell Bleachworks	1739	Smithills Croft Road, Bolton	6960 1134	Ainsworths
Astley Brook				
17 Sharples Bleachworks	1821/2	Sharples	7095 1132	Eden & Thwaites
River Tonge				
18 Little Bolton Bleachworks	1836	Slater Lane, Bolton	7206 1022	James & John Slater
19 Mill Hill Bleachworks	1821/2	Kestor Street, Bolton	7256 0973	George Blair
Doffcocker Brook				
20 Mortfield Bleachworks	1821/2	Mortfield Lane, Bolton	7073 0993	Rothwell, then Thos. Cross
Middlebrook/River Croal				
21 Gilnow Bleachworks	1821/2	Gilnow Road, Bolton	7032 0879	Ainsworths, then William Makant
22 Bolton Bleachworks	1821/2	Chorley Street, Bolton	7111 0929	Bridson, Ridgway
23 Ridgway's Bleachcroft	before 1777	Ridgway Gates, Bolton	approx 715 094	James Ridgway
24 Burnden Bleachworks	1750	Burnden Road, Bolton	7273 0812	Roger Holland
25 Raikes Lane Bleachworks	c. 1788	Raikes Lane, Bolton	7327 0788	Horridge & Holmes
26 Great Lever Bleachworks	1795	Smith's Road, Bolton	7350 0747	John Smith Jnr
27 Farnworth Bleachworks	1894	Hall Lane, Farnworth	7447 0679	J.B. Champion & Co.
River Irwell				
28 Lever Bank Bleachworks	c. 1831	nr Ladyshore, Little Lever	7621 0637	Bridsons, then John Smith Jnr
29 Mount Sion Bleachworks	before 1859	Mount Sion Road, Radcliffe	767 067	John Whittaker

continued overleaf

	Title	Date	Location	Map ref. (all SD)	Name of Firm
	Pearl (Purl) Brook				
30	Wallsuches Bleachworks	1777	Wallsuches, Horwich	6539 1177	Ridgways
31	Horwich Bleachworks, Horwich	*c.* 1770	Bridge Street, then Longworth	644 117	France & Pass
	River Douglas				
32	Knoll Bleachworks	before 1795	Shaws Wood, Horwich	642 128	Ridgway?
33	Star Vale Bleach & Dyeworks	*c.* 1860	Star Lane, Horwich	627 112	Whitecroft plc
34	Huyton Bleachworks	1812	Huyton Road, Adlington	6073 1277	Gallimore & Liddell, then Davies & Eckersley
	Blackshaw Brook				
35	Breightmet Bleachworks	*c.* 1779	Redbridge, Breightmet	7516 0993	Seddon, then Constantine & Ormrod
36	Ainsworth Mercerising	*c.* 1890	Bury Road, Breightmet	7524 0941	Nathan Ramsden & Co.

(See also map of sites on page 41.)

Chapter 8

WATER POWER IN BOLTON

T he harnessing of flowing water to turn a waterwheel is one of the earliest uses of a natural power source. One of the first applications of water power was to rotate a pair of circular grindstones to grind corn into flour between the opposing flat faces. Another was to pound newly woven woollen cloth in an alkaline liquor under large swinging mallets or stocks to thicken and tighten up the weave of the material, a process called fulling. A set of water-powered fulling stocks of 1850 can be seen working in the Higher Mill Textile Museum, Helmshore.

Several corn and fulling mills were situated on local streams around Bolton. Records show that a corn mill using water from the Bradshaw Brook was in existence in 1542. Although no longer there today, it ceased working in 1806 and is known to be sited in the Jumbles (SD7346 1379).[1] Another corn mill, known as Rumworth Mill, was recorded in 1592 on the Middlebrook, but its exact site is unknown.[2] Smithills Corn Mill on the Dean Brook, built before 1620, was at SD6971 133, but the site is now covered by houses; some ashlar stones lie in the stream and they may be all that remain today.[3] A document of 1635 records a corn mill and drying kiln owned by a Lawrence Brownlowe of Tonge.[4] Presumably the mill was sited somewhere on the River Tonge. Bradshaw Brook also powered Turton Corn Mill (SD738 158); it was working when sold to Humphrey Chetham in 1628.[5] There was a working fulling mill on Eagley Brook as early as 1483[6] and another on Bradshaw Brook in 1542,[7] but their exact sites are not known today. A water-powered corn mill was also sited on Hardy Mill Road.[8] The origin of all these mills probably lies in the old manorial system.

The need for fulling mills in the area had declined by about 1700, as Bolton had concentrated on cotton spinning by this date. Corn mills continued in use until much later. The next new application of water power was for driving cotton preparation and spinning machinery in the new cotton mills, from about 1780. No waterwheels survive from these early water-powered mills, but traces of the original water supply and discharge systems do exist. The most common feature is the reservoir or mill pond, built to give a reserve supply of water in periods of drought. Other surviving remains often include a long near-level headrace or leat, to bring river water to the wheel from a point upstream, and a weir to provide an adequate head of water for the wheel. An example may be seen in the Jumbles Valley, where a long leat used to bring water to Bradshaw Bleachworks from a point higher up the Bradshaw Brook. Short tailraces returning water back into the river may still be seen in some places, such as at St Helena Mill. Spillways may be found along a headrace to allow excess water to escape in times of flooding. Wheel pits (open or filled in) still survive in

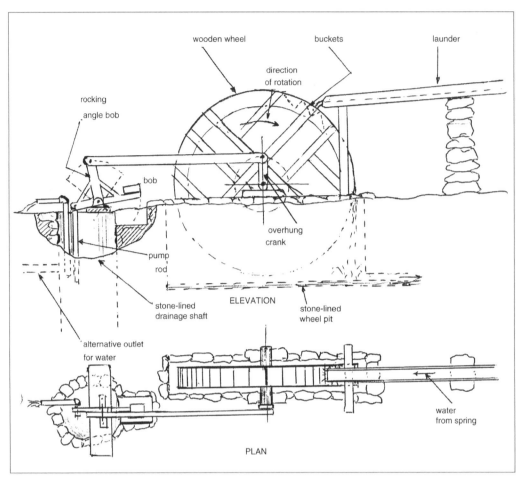

A sketch of Limestone Clough waterwheel. *(Author's Collection)*

places, such as the open pit at the lead workings in Lead Mines Valley[9] (see Chapter 14), or the filled-in one at Egerton Mill, which once held a 62ft-diameter iron wheel. An 1848 engraving of that wheel has appeared in several books,[10] and for a period of nearly twenty years this was the largest wheel in the country, only exceeded by the Laxey Wheel in the Isle of Man. The Egerton wheel was designed by Johann Georg Bodmer (1786–1864), a Swiss engineer living in Bolton. Rothwell, Hick & Rothwell began construction in 1828, but owing to financial problems the wheel was not finished until 1835, by Fairbairn & Lillie of Manchester. Owing to an irregular water supply from the Eagley Brook, the wheel became a white elephant, and was replaced by steam power in the 1850s. The wheel pit was not filled in until the early 1980s. All that remains today are two pulleys and some iron castings built into the walls.

However, one waterwheel does survive, which came from what was once Rostron's Spinning Mill (formerly Turton Corn Mill). In 1853 a new iron wheel replaced an existing wooden one, and in about 1890 the site became Black Brook Bleach & Dye Works. In 1917 the buildings were demolished, leaving the wheel *in situ* covered in rubble. It was rescued by members of the Turton Local History Society in 1976, restored and resited in 1980 in a specially prepared wheel pit outside Turton Tower stables. The wheel measures 13ft 10½in outside diameter by 6ft 1in wide, high breast, with a Rennie patent sliding hatch penstock. It is a suspension wheel with power taken off a rim gear. Another small breast-shot wheel from Old Hall Farm, Heaton,[11] which originally powered a butter churn, is now at the Lakeland Mine and Quarry Museum, Threlkeld. Rivington Hall also once had a small overshot waterwheel. It has been estimated that in 1838, 21 per cent of the total horsepower used by Bolton's mills was produced by water, and some mills were still using water as late as the 1860s.[12]

A few miles down the Irwell Valley is an important industrial archaeological site at Clifton, Wet Earth Colliery, where James Brindley (1716–72) used water from the Irwell

A sketch of Edgerton Mill's waterwheel. The wheel, at 62ft in diameter, was an engineering wonder of the day. People came from near and far to see it. Made in Bolton in 1835, it ran until 1868 when it was replaced by steam power. *(Author's Collection)*

Waterwheel from Black Rock Bleachworks. Rescued by Turton Local History Society, the wheel was resited in the grounds of Turton Tower. *(Author's Collection)*

to drive pumps that de-watered the mine. The pumps were driven by a wooden breast-shot type waterwheel, located in a brick chamber some 20ft below ground. The wheel no longer exists – it was taken out in 1867 – but from the marks on the wall it was probably about 22ft in diameter. Cranks operated vertical reciprocating pump rods, which powered bucket pumps working 150ft down the adjoining Gal Pit.[13]

To bring water to the wheel, Brindley built a weir upstream from the colliery, near Ringley Fold. Water from above the weir was brought through a tunnel on the opposite (north) side of the river. The supply was transferred to the other bank by an inverted syphon constructed below the bed of the river, a method which was unique at that date. Water was discharged from the syphon into an open leat or feeder channel, which ran alongside the Irwell for a further 2,000ft, and then turned away from the river into a short tunnel which led to the wheel chamber. After turning the wheel, the water entered an underground tailrace which brought it back to the river bank, at that point some 30ft below the level of the pithead. Water pumped out of the mine was discharged into the same tailrace. Work on the scheme started in 1752, and was completed by 1756, when pumping began. The waterwheel was replaced in 1867 by a low-pressure water turbine using the same water supply and exit arrangements. The turbine ran until 1924, when it was scrapped, and the colliery finally closed in 1928.

In 1790 a mining engineer, Matthew Fletcher (1731–1808), extended Brindley's feeder channel as a navigable narrow canal from Wet Earth Colliery to join the Manchester, Bolton & Bury Canal at Clifton aqueduct. A branch from this canal led to Botany Bay Colliery, and the water from this supplied a waterwheel that drove winding gear for raising coal from the pit bottom. After leaving the wheel, the water returned to the Irwell.

Brindley's feeder channel is silted up today, but its route can be traced, and a number of original features remain. The inverted syphon is sealed off for safety reasons, as is the tailrace exit. The whole area is in the Croal-Irwell Valley Country Park. Many other colliery drainage adits can be found in the riverbank, and some of these have been dug out and surveyed by the Wet Earth Colliery Exploration Group, though Salford City Council has has closed the site and refuses to allow access.

A further example of the use of water power can be seen in the rusting remains of a low-pressure water turbine dating from the late nineteenth century. This is built into the south bank of the Irwell at SD7757 0433. Water from Brindley's feeder channel was led down a large-diameter pipe to the turbine, which drove a pump forcing water from the river up to a higher level to supply a coal-washing plant.

The earliest waterwheels were of massive wooden construction. The torque generated by the water acting on the buckets was transmitted by heavy radial arms down to the central axle, which was connected by the gearing to drive machinery. In about 1770 stronger cast-iron axles were introduced, and by the early nineteenth century wrought-iron rims, iron arms and curved sheet-iron buckets were common. Near the end of the century, lightweight iron wheels were invented with a large diameter cast-iron gear bolted onto the rim in sections, from which power was taken off through a small pinion. This construction eliminated the need for torque transmitting arms, and comparatively slender spokes were substituted. The wheel therefore behaved like a bicycle wheel, and was known as a suspension or tension wheel. The design enabled large-diameter wheels to be made, such as the Egerton wheel. The power a waterwheel can develop depends on its diameter and width, the point where the water enters the circumference, and the velocity of the incoming water.

Some waterwheels were sited against an outside wall of the building they served; others were placed inside, sometimes in a special outbuilding. The owner of a waterwheel had a legal right to use water from the river (the riparian right), and if any reduction in flow occurred due to some man-made interference upstream, compensation water had to be sent downstream to maintain the quantity of water. The biggest problem with water power was the lack of water that could occur from natural causes. Summer drought or winter freezing could reduce or stop a mill working. Millponds or reservoirs storing water against such conditions alleviated the problem, but records show that water-powered mills were sometimes out of action for several weeks during particularly dry summers.

Chapter 9

STEAM POWER IN BOLTON

The earliest steam engines had overhead rocking beams, which operated vertical pumps positioned down mineshafts to drain the underground workings. James Watt (1736–1819) developed the engine, and by 1779 had invented a rotative version in which the rocking motion of the beam turned an output shaft. Rotary motion greatly increased the usefulness of the engines, since they could drive many types of machinery. Non-rotative beam engines continued to be used for many years on pumping duties, particularly by public water companies for pumping water and for sewage disposal.

Although Watt had protected his design of engine and condenser by a patent, which did not expire until 1800, many engines were made illegally to his design before the patent expired. Several of these were made in Manchester. Mill owners soon saw the advantages of steam power, the main ones being that mills could be sited virtually anywhere within easy reach of coal, and that a steam mill was not dependant on a river as a source of power, as is one driven by a waterwheel. Furthermore, year-round operation was possible. Mills and factories came to be built on cheap land away from the river, on the outskirts of the town.

In some cases a steam engine was added to an existing waterwheel installation to pump water from the wheel's tailrace back onto the buckets. Recirculating the water allowed the wheel to keep turning during times when the river was low, so there was no interruption of production. The mill would otherwise be stopped while the wheel was taken out and an engine put in. Carlisle's Mill, built in 1787 in Bolling Yard off Bradshawgate (now demolished), was an example.[1] New Eagley Mill also had a recirculating steam engine in 1831, and there were other examples.

According to James Clegg, one of Bolton's local historians, writing in 1888, the first cotton mill in Bolton to use steam power exclusively was in 1790, but he does not say where.[2] Nor is it known if the engine was a Newcomen type, a Boulton & Watt or an illegal copy. Wallsuches Bleachworks had a 10hp Boulton & Watt engine in 1798. By September 1825 there were eighty-three steam engines in Bolton and the vicinity, totalling 1,604hp.[3]

Rotative beam engines continued to drive mills, factories, forges, and so on, well into the nineteenth century. By about 1850 direct-acting horizontal engines were being built, the size increasing as larger and larger mills were built. Later high-speed inverted vertical engines[4] were developed, particularly by John Musgrave & Sons. In the heyday of the mill-type horizontal engine, some as powerful as 3,000hp were in use in cotton mills and for winding coal at pit-heads. Some early twentieth-century mills had steam turbines rather than reciprocating steam engines. These turned generators that supplied electricity to large electric motors driving lineshafting on each floor of the mill. Kearsley Mill and Falcon Mill are examples of this.

Although mill engines remain *in situ* in some towns, notably Wigan and Milnrow, none do in Bolton. All engines in Bolton cotton mills were scrapped as the mills closed down or were demolished. The engines in the Northern Mill Engine Society's collection were brought in from outside the town – even the one example which is Bolton built. The Society has a database listing details of the engines that once provided power for local mills, from a range of makers.

Reminders of steam power can still be seen in mills and factories. Mill lodges were originally used to cool the hot water from the engine condenser, and these sometimes remain. A very few still hold water, but most have been filled in for safety, and often turned into car parks for the firms that occupy them now. The factory or mill chimney may still be standing, though many have been felled or reduced in height. At one time Bolton's skyline was dotted with tall chimneys, each emitting its plume of smoke. These often carried the name of the mill or firm for advertising purposes. The boilerhouse was sited near the base of the chimney. The boilers in this generated steam for the engine, and for space heating or process work. Boilerhouses can be identified as single-storey, purely functional buildings, usually with some form of ventilation in the roof. Early steam boilers were of the wagon type, and could only generate low-pressure steam. By the mid-nineteenth century Lancashire boilers had become the universal steam raisers used in mills, generating pressures up to 200psi by the end of the century. Large mills had banks of Lancashire boilers. Swan Lane Mills, for example, had ten boilers, with one always on standby.

Mill engine houses are usually distinctive, as it was the custom to give them special architectural embellishment such as large, arched, church-like windows with carved stone decorations and tiled interiors. Sometimes it is possible to determine which type of engine the building once housed. Large, wide engine houses of only modest height most likely held horizontal engines. Beam engines needed a greater height, so a taller building with a smaller plan area in an older mill probably held one or two beam engines. This is not conclusive, as a tall engine house in a later mill, or a newer engine house added to an older mill, may have held an inverted vertical type of engine, possibly replacing the original beam engine. Engine houses may be external to a mill or projecting from the main mill building, or they may be integral to it. Atlas Mills Nos 1, 2, 3 and 4 were originally powered by beam engines in integral engine houses, but these were replaced in Mills 3 and 4 by large inverted vertical engines in new projecting engine houses, early in the twentieth century. These mills have been largely demolished, and Morrison's supermarket occupies the site. A large horizontal engine in an engine house close to Chorley Old Road powered the surviving Atlas Mill No. 6, and through lineshafting the adjacent mill, No. 7. The Atlas Mills were built by James Musgrave, and all the engines used here were built by his father's firm, John Musgrave & Sons.

As steam engines developed over the years, power output increased, higher working pressures were used, and engineering techniques improved. As steam expands in a cylinder, its temperature falls and it may start to condense, which reduces the power. As boiler working pressures increased, compound engines became common, in which the steam expands in two stages, initially in a high-pressure cylinder and then in a large lower-pressure cylinder, before being exhausted to the condenser. In the late nineteenth century triple-expansion engines came into use, with separate high-, intermediate- and low-pressure cylinders.

The engines in many of the mills of the Bolton district were built by local engineering firms. The three main engine builders in Bolton were Hick Hargreaves & Co., John Musgrave & Sons, and J. & E. Wood. No Bolton-built engines remain on their original sites in the town, but several have been preserved elsewhere, including:

1. A horizontal cross-compound engine of 450hp, 75rpm, steam pressure 125psi, built by J. & E. Wood, is on static display near India Mill, Darwen. Built in 1906, it ran until 1970.

Cross-compound horizontal mill engine of 1905, by J. & E. Wood of Bolton. *(Author's Collection)*

Inverted vertical mill engine of 1913 in the Northern Mill Engine Society's steam museum, Bolton. *(Author's Collection)*

2. A horizontal tandem compound engine, also by J. & E. Wood, is preserved by Bolton Museum, currently in store.
3. A 2,500hp four-cylinder triple expansion engine by J. & E. Wood (two low-pressure cylinders), built in 1907, 68rpm, is preserved *in situ* at Trencherfield Mill, Wigan (part of the Wigan Pier site). This ran until 1967, and is one of the largest engines built.
4. An inverted vertical single-cylinder engine of 150hp, 88rpm, built in 1886 with Inglis valve gear by Hick Hargreaves, ran until 1969 in a silk-weaving mill at Low Bentham, North Yorkshire. It was presented to the town by the makers, and is preserved in a glass case in Oxford Street in the town centre, rotated by an electric motor.
5. A 'non-dead-centre' engine by John Musgrave & Sons (a two-cylinder inverted vertical compound design), 150hp, 120rpm, built in 1893, is in the Northern Mill Engine Society's collection, housed in the old no. 4 cotton store, Atlas Mills. This came from a mill in Radcliffe and is an unusual design, originally developed for

Twin-beam mill engines, *c.* 1840, in the Northern Mill Engine Society's steam museum. *(Author's Collection)*

marine use, and is believed to be the only surviving engine of its type. The Society is working towards eventually opening the building as the Bolton Steam Museum.

The Northern Mill Engine Society has a wide range of engines dating from about 1840 to 1933, from various makers, at its Atlas Mills site.[5] The frontplate of a Hick Hargreaves Lancashire boiler, rescued from Halliwell Mill, Bolton, is included in its collection. Complete Lancashire boilers can be seen at Quarry Bank Mill, Styal, and Ellen Road Mill, Milnrow, and a Galloway boiler (a development of the Lancashire boiler) is preserved at the Museum of Science and Industry in Manchester.

In 1840 Benjamin Hick built for Marshall's flax mill in Leeds a twin-beam engine of 120hp, running on 15psi steam pressure. A $\frac{1}{10}$ size working model of the engine was made and exhibited at the 1851 Great Exhibition in London, and may be seen today in the Science Museum, South Kensington.

A steam-powered item from a non-textile industry that has been preserved is the double-acting shingling hammer,[6] which was formerly in Walmesley's Atlas Forge (now demolished), Fletcher Street, Bolton. Walmesley's produced wrought iron in Bolton for over 100 years. The hammer is on permanent display in front of Bolton University, Deane Road. The complete forge – steam-powered rolling mill, furnaces, and so on – has been re-erected in the Blists Hill Open Air Museum at Ironbridge, Shropshire, and the making of wrought iron by the old puddling process is demonstrated there from time to time.

Electricity was generated in Bolton by steam raised in coal-fired power stations from the late 1890s up until the mid-1980s. When electric trams started running in 1899, a direct-current supply was generated in the Spa Road station using Musgrave engines driving 550-volt dynamos. A smaller station was also opened in Albert Road, Farnworth.

A public three-phase alternating current supply at 460/240 volts was generated from 1923 to 1979 at Back o' th' Bank power station. A turbine and generator from here have been re-erected at the Museum of Science and Industry in Manchester. A larger station was opened at Kearsley in 1929, which ran until 1985, when it too was demolished. In both stations electricity was generated by steam-driven turbo-alternators.

A small Bolton-built vertical engine, used for driving machines in engineering workshops. *(Author's Collection)*

The front of a hand-fired Lancashire boiler, the most popular type of steam raiser in mills and factories. *(Author's Collection)*

A steam-powered shingling hammer from Walmsley's Atlas Forge, resited outside Bolton University. *(Author's Collection)*

Another important use of steam power was of course the locomotive. Bolton firms supplied locomotives for the Bolton & Leigh Railway, which opened officially in 1828. In 1830 Rothwell, Hick & Rothwell built the *Union* locomotive, which ran on the line for many years. The following year Crook & Dean built two locomotives, the *Salamander* and the *Veteran*. In 1834 Benjamin Hick & Sons built the *Soho* for the line. Bolton firms continued building locomotives up to about 1860, many for overseas railways. During the years 1884–7 the Lancashire & Yorkshire Railway built their new works on Chorley New Road at Horwich. Here steam locomotives were built and repaired from 1889 until 1962.

A conical rope drum and brake of a reversible steam-winding engine at a colliery pit head. *(Author's Collection)*

Sans Pareil locomotive. After the Rainhill trials of 1829 this locomotive ran on the Bolton & Leigh Railway for eleven years. *(Author's Collection)*

A canalside steam-operated crane with integral boiler. *(Author's Collection)*

During the early years of the Bolton & Leigh Railway stationary steam engines were needed to pull locomotives and their trains up inclines at Daubhill and Chequerbent. When locomotives became powerful enough to climb the gradients unaided, the stationary engines and winding gear were scrapped.

Eventually electric power superseded steam power in mills and factories, and the steam engine became part of our industrial heritage. Steam has a great fascination for many – particularly steam locomotives, which keep the memory of these prime movers alive today.

Chapter 10

THE ENGINEERING INDUSTRY

IN BOLTON

After textiles, engineering was the major industry and a large employer in Bolton during the nineteenth century. Items manufactured included waterwheels, boilers and stationary steam engines, textile machinery and mill equipment, locomotives, railway rolling stock, and all manner of capital goods.

Mechanical engineering developed during the course of the Industrial Revolution as power-driven, machine-made artefacts gradually replaced the old hand-crafted ones. The skills of the carpenter, blacksmith and millwright were replaced by machine tools, which were developed and perfected to achieve greater precision than the traditional hand methods. During the years known as the 'Railway Mania' (c. 1840–60), a professional class of engineers emerged, marked by the formation of the Institution of Mechanical Engineers in 1847, with George Stephenson as its first president. John Hick of Hick Hargreaves, Crook Street, Bolton, was a founder member of the Institution.[1] By this date Hick's had been building locomotives for several years.

The pioneers of Bolton's engineering industry were first active in the last quarter of the eighteenth century, responding to the demand for metal parts for the cotton preparation and spinning machinery installed in the new mills of the period. Brief histories of some of the principal engineering concerns are outlined below.

The firm of Dobson & Rothwell was founded in 1790, and eventually developed into the large, well-known textile machinery manufacturers, Dobson & Barlow. Isaac Dobson (1767–1833), a farmer from Patterdale, Cumbria, set up a small engineering works in Blackhorse Street in the centre of Bolton, in partnership with Peter Rothwell (1755–1816), a Bolton timber merchant, to make hand-operated mules. It was a suitable partnership, as contemporary mules had wooden frames and only the highly stressed or rotating parts were made of metal – either iron or brass. Their factory was first powered by a horse gin, which drove lathes and drilling machines.[2] No traces of this early works remain today. The firm prospered, and in 1846 transferred to a larger site in Kay Street, then on the outskirts of the town, occupying Blinkhorn's former chemical works. In 1851 Edward Barlow (1821–68) joined the firm, which became Dobson & Barlow. During the years at Kay Street, Dobson & Barlow developed their renowned self-acting mule, which was capable of spinning the finest yarns. By 1890 the company was employing around 4,000 men. In 1906 the firm moved to Bradley Fold, just out of the Bolton area in Bury township, and the Kay Street works became B. & F. Carter. The company name survived until 1970, when it became a

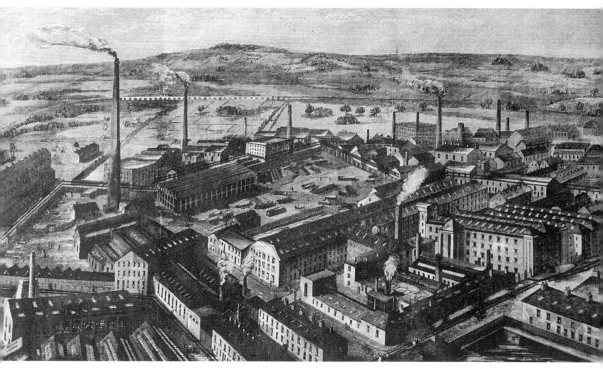

Dobson & Barlow engineering works, 1873. *(Bolton Evening News)*

part of Platt International, following a take-over by Platts of Oldham, another well-known firm of textile machinery makers. The firm finally closed in 1984, but some of the buildings still exist on the Bradley Fold site.

Examples of Dobson & Barlow textile machines can be seen at Higher Mill Museum, Helmshore, and in the Museum of Science and Industry in Manchester. A fine spinning mule is held in store by Bolton Museum, and may be exhibited at a future date. A statue of Sir Benjamin Alfred Dobson (1847–98), a fourth-generation descendant of the founder of the firm, stands in Victoria Square in front of the town hall. He was a managing director and four times mayor of Bolton.

Another early engineering firm that had its beginnings in Blackhorse Street was the Union foundry of Smalley, Thwaites & Co., founded in about 1801, which made water-wheels, boilers and beam engines. In 1815 Benjamin Hick (1790–1842) came from Yorkshire to join the company, which then became Thwaites, Hick & Rothwell, and later, in 1825, Rothwell, Hick & Rothwell. The second Rothwell was Peter (1792–1849), son of the first. In 1830 the firm built the *Union* locomotive, designed by Benjamin Hick, for the new Bolton & Leigh Railway. Three years later Hick left the firm to start up his own works, the Soho Ironworks in Crook Street. The Union foundry then became Rothwell & Co. until it was taken over in about 1924 by the nearby Bolton Iron & Steel Co. During its history the Union foundry built about 200 steam locomotives. The site was cleared in 1927, and is now occupied by the bus station and market. An old weighbridge platform which survives near the Doffcocker toll-house still carries the name Rothwell, Hick & Rothwell.

One old engineering firm, which was taken over by BOC Edwards in August 2002, is Hick Hargreaves of Crook Street, Bolton. As mentioned above, Benjamin Hick founded the firm in 1833 with his two sons, choosing the name Soho ironworks, possibly copied from the famous factory of Boulton & Watt in Birmingham. In 1834 they built their first locomotive, the *Soho*, for the Bolton & Leigh Railway. The firm also made boilers, beam engines, mill transmission systems, and so on. In 1845 John Hick (1815–94) succeeded his father, who had died three years previously, and took John and William Hargreaves into partnership; John Hargreaves was goods traffic manager on the Bolton & Leigh Railway, and William was his son. The firm became known as Hick Hargreaves, and still carries the same title today. Many locomotives were built for British railways, and some for railways in France, the last one being built in 1855. In 1850 the firm began to build marine engines, as well as horizontal-type mill engines; in the late 1870s manufacture of refrigeration equipment commenced.[3] By the 1890s some 1,500 stationary steam engines had been built, ranging from 40hp to 4,000hp. In the early twentieth century, uniflow engines, steam turbines, air compressors and oil engines were produced, as the demand for mill-type steam engines fell with the decline of the cotton trade. John Hick was elected as MP for Bolton in 1868 and resigned from the firm; William Hargreaves carried on.

Some of the original buildings remain on the Crook Street site, together with fine turn-of-the-century machine and erecting shops. A Hick Hargreaves single-cylinder inverted vertical engine is displayed in a glass case in Oxford Street, in the town centre; a single-cylinder horizontal engine is preserved at the Forncett Industrial Museum, near Norwich. Scale models of some of their engines may also be seen in Bolton Museum, which also has many original drawings of the company's early locomotives on loan from the company, drawn by Benjamin Hick and his son John. Portraits of John Hick and his wife hang on the walls of the foyer of the Museum & Art Gallery.

Richard Threlfall (1804–68), James Spencer and John Sutcliffe founded the company of Richard Threlfall & Co. in 1834, and a chimney carrying the company's name survives on the site of the original works in Bridgeman Place, Salop Street. Richard had worked at Dobson & Barlow's, and the firm made textile machinery, principally spinning mules. Richard was in full control of the company from 1838 until his death in 1868. The company was then run by trustees for fifteen years, until William Hurst (1859–1906), Richard's son-in-law, became proprietor. The company has remained in the Hurst family up to the present day. Threlfall's Bolton-style fine spinning mules were highly regarded, and large numbers were made, many for export worldwide. By 1940 the company was making ring spinning machines, and when the textile trade declined, was able to diversify. Today specialised valves are produced for the Ministry of Defence and the off-shore gas industry,[4] but the original site is in multiple occupation.

Two well-known builders of stationary steam engines were John Musgrave & Sons and J. & E. Wood, who between them equipped many mills in Bolton and elsewhere. John Musgrave & Sons was founded in 1839 by John Musgrave (1784–1864), who had worked at Hick's Soho ironworks. He took over Daly's Globe ironworks in Kay Street, next to Blinkhorn's Little Bolton chemical works, and began to manufacture engines of all kinds – beam engines at first, then vertical colliery winding engines, horizontal mill engines, and later inverted vertical and uniflow engines, which were exported to Japan, Russia and India. In 1851 suspension chains were made for the 2,400ft-span bridge across the River Dnieper in Russia.[5] James Musgrave, John's son, diversified into cotton spinning, building the Atlas Mills Complex in Chorley Old Road from 1864. John Musgrave & Sons produced all the metal parts for the mills – cast-iron pillars, and so on – and equipped them with their own engines. They were an early supplier of mill rope drives, and later specialised in building large inverted vertical mill engines, one of which survives in the collection of the Northern Mill Engine Society, housed in the old no. 4 cotton store on the Atlas Mills site. This is a twin-cylinder compound non-dead-centre 1893 inverted vertical engine of 150hp. A horizontal tandem compound Musgrave engine of 1907 is preserved at the works of the Carbolite Co. at Bamford in Derbyshire.

John and Edward Wood began to build engines at their Victoria Foundry in Garside Street in about 1860. They made beam, vertical and horizontal compound engines, condensing and non-condensing, in all sizes up to 2,500hp. Three J. & E. Wood engines survive: a small cross-compound preserved outside India Mill, Darwen, a large four-cylinder triple-expansion engine in Trencherfield Mill, Wigan (part of the Wigan Pier complex), and a tandem compound stored by Bolton Museum. They also made hydraulic presses, turbines, mill gearing, and gas-making equipment, and undertook all kinds of general engineering work for home and overseas customers. The company had closed by 1912; part of the site is now occupied by Rigby Taylor (Paints) Ltd, and some of the original buildings survive.

William Crook and John Dean founded the general engineering company Crook & Dean in about 1826 in Folds Road, Bolton. In 1831 they built a locomotive, *The Phoenix*, named after their ironworks, and in about 1840 another locomotive, *The Salamander*, both for the Bolton & Leigh Railway. Little is known about the firm, and by about 1860 it had ceased to exist. The site of the works is near the point where St Peter's Way crosses Folds Road.

Wharf Foundry, Well Street, Bolton, was near the former terminus of the Bolton arm of the Manchester, Bolton & Bury Canal, and was founded by the Jackson Brothers in 1792. Initially they made equipment for bleachworks and the textile industry. When orders for the textile industry declined, Jackson Brothers turned to other kinds of engineering and foundry work, finally specialising in the repair of centrifugal pumps. The company later became part of the engineering firm Mather & Platt of Manchester, and before it closed in 1977 claimed to be the oldest engineering works in Bolton still occupying its original site.[6]

John Booth & Sons, general and structural engineers, occupied a rebuilt cotton mill in Back King Street, in the town centre, adjoining the River Croal, in 1872. From 1802 to 1815, Samuel Crompton rented the attic of the original 1797 building, where he operated two of his mules. An old photograph shows that the building carried a large painted notice announcing this occupancy, until the attic was removed in 1928.[7] The rest of the building has subsequently been demolished and the site redeveloped. In 1906 Booth's acquired a twenty-acre site on St Helen's Road as its main Hulton steelworks where it also had railway sidings. Later the town centre works was given up. At the St Helen's Road site there was a machine shop, a large fabrication shop, and steam-operated cranes in the yard.[8] After occupying this site for eighty-nine years, Booth's gave up structural steelwork and moved to a smaller site in Nelson Street, Great Lever, to concentrate on specialised engineering work. It took over the works of Entwistle & Gass, which had been in business since 1852, and latterly made hydraulic presses and injection moulding machines, before going into liquidation in 1994. The St Helen's Road site is now a housing estate.

Thomas Mitchell & Sons of Edgar Street, off Fletcher Street, is a firm of engineers' merchants still operating on a site it has occupied since the early twentieth century. The main machine shops and offices were purpose-built at that time; the four main storage bays were converted from a short street of terraced houses by removing all the internal walls and roofing over the shells of the two terraces, the street between, and the back alley behind one row. The firm was originally founded in 1838 on a site now covered by the town hall. In their early years the firm supplied stationary steam engines, boilers and locomotives, new or second-hand, machine tools and millwrighting items such as shafting, bearings, pulleys and gears. The site is still crammed with old machinery of all kinds, including several steam engines and generating sets. In 1984 it supplied two Robey steam engines – a cross-compound and a uniflow – to the Northern Mill Engine Society. Its main business today is reconditioning and supplying electric motors and pumps.

Horwich Locomotive Works, Chorley New Road, was the second locomotive works built by the old Lancashire & Yorkshire Railway, replacing the original works in Miles Platting, Manchester. Horwich works opened officially in 1886. It became an LMS works at the grouping in 1923, and part of British Railways on nationalisation in 1947. The works was specifically designed for the manufacture and repair of steam locomotives, being laid out in five parallel lines of single-storey brick sheds, with cast-iron stanchions supporting the roof and 30-ton overhead travelling cranes. Standard-gauge rail tracks were laid out inside the buildings, with a connection to the nearby L. & Y. Bolton to Preston line.

The first locomotive built at Horwich – no. 1,008, a 2–4–2 radial tank designed by John Aspinall (1851–1937) – left the works in 1889. It was one of a batch of ten, and has been preserved in the National Railway Museum, York.[9] The works originally contained a boiler-making and repair shop, foundry and forge, machine tool and fitters' shops, and an erecting and repair shop over 1,500ft long, together with other support and servicing shops, drawing office and general office. An 18in-gauge works transport system worked by small steam locomotives serviced the various sheds to facilitate the movement of materials around the site.[10] By 1894 some 3,000 men were employed at the works, rising to 4,200 in 1921. During its lifetime Horwich works constructed 1,835 standard-gauge steam locomotives.[11] Over the years alterations to the layout and modernisation took place, to suit changes made in the type of work undertaken. Diesel locomotives were built after 1957, and the last steam locomotive was repaired in 1964. From then on the works concentrated on carriage and wagon repairs, and overhauling electric multiple units, until closure in December 1983. Most of the original buildings still stand today, now occupied by various small concerns, mostly engineering firms. The L. & Y. Railway built a small cottage-type hospital adjoining their works in Chorley New Road. It was demolished some years ago, but a scale model made by Mr E. Richardson of Bolton is held by the Horwich Heritage Local History Society.

The factory of James Baxendale & Sons, founded in 1856 on Pilkington Street, off Derby Street, claimed to be the largest of its type in Lancashire. The firm made all kinds of items in tin plate, sheet-iron and copper, for cotton mills, bleachers, brewers and engineering firms. The works contained a large workshop in three bays, one of which had second-floor offices. James Baxendale invented and patented several improvements to machinery for cotton spinning.

Engineering works of the nineteenth and early twentieth centuries are not very distinctive in appearance, and usually did not have much architectural merit. One exception is the architect-designed Horwich locomotive works. They were usually simple functional buildings, built of brick or stone. They were mainly single-storey structures, except for the offices. Workshops had pitched roofs with overhead glazing, often with ventilators spaced out along the roof or a continuous run of louvres, especially where the processes occurring below produced large amounts of heat, as with metal casting. The site would contain several buildings of different sizes, each one housing a specific process or function – machine tools, foundry, erecting shop, and so on. One or two brick or metal chimneys served small boilers which supplied steam for space heating and for small steam engines, which drove lineshafts for the various machine tools. Most buildings had large doors, sliding or roller-shutter type, which opened onto the factory yard. Overhead travelling cranes allowed large objects and heavy weights to be lifted and moved around the workshops. Sometimes the travelling crane extended out over the factory yard. Large works, such as Hick Hargreaves, Soho ironworks and the Bolton Steel Co., had private sidings from nearby railway lines which entered the yard, with connections leading into most workshops via turntables.

The opening of Bolton Mechanics' Institute. The Institute was officially opened by the author Anthony Trollope. A Hugon gas engine was on display, the first internal combustion engine seen in Bolton. *(Bolton Evening News)*

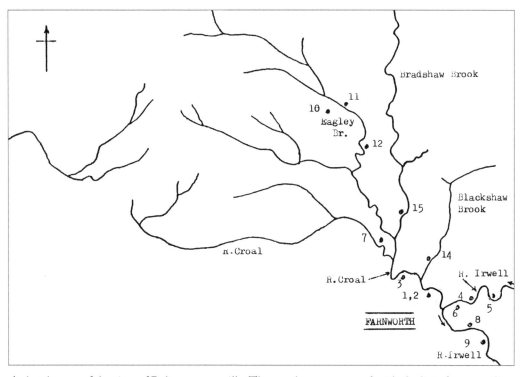

A sketch map of the sites of Bolton paper mills. The numbers correspond with the list of paper mills. *(Author's Collection)*

BOLTON AND DISTRICT PAPER MAKERS

No. on map	Name of paper mill	River or stream	Map ref. (all SD)	Date mill founded	Founding owner or occupier	Comments
1	Darley Hall, Farnworth	Croal	7447 0679	*c.* 1687	Robert Crompton (*c.* 1667–1737)	Ceased working *c.* 1737.
2	Farnworth Bridge	Croal	7447 0679	*c.* 1783	Ellis Crompton (1729–1803)	Became Champion's Bleachworks 1894. Demolished 1970s.
3	Great Lever	Croal	7350 0747	1726	Ellis Crompton (1693–1760)	Became bleachworks.
4	Creams, Little Lever	Irwell	7570 0637	1677	James Crompton (*c.* 1646–1704)	Still working as Danisco Paper.
5	Grundy's (Leadbeater's), Little Lever	Irwell	7623 0637	before 1783	John Grundy (d. *c.* 1830)	Ceased *c.* 1830. Became bleachworks.
6	Seddon's, Prestolee Bridge	Irwell	Possibly 7524 0627	Working 1707	Robert Seddon	Demolished, no trace.

continued overleaf

No. on map	Name of paper mill	River or stream	Map ref. (all SD)	Date mill founded	Founding owner or occupier	Comments
7	Springfield, Bolton	Croal	7234 0862	1820	John Livesey Jnr (b. 1786)	Now Trinity Retail Park.
8	Dyehouse, Prestolee	Irwell	Possibly 7523 0563	before 1788	John Livesey Snr (b. 1744)	Ceased *c.* 1825.
9	Stoneclough	Irwell	7589 0562	1823	Ralph Crompton	Became Robert Fletcher's in 1859. Still working.
10	Spring Side, off Belmont Road	Eagley Brook	6925 1508	1834	John Livesey Jnr (b. 1786)	Still working as Charles Turner.
11	Eagley	Eagley Brook	7216 1295	*c.* 1849	Knowles & Crook	Closed 1884. Site demolished.
12	Hall i' th' Wood	Eagley Brook	7213 1161	*c.* 1816	Thomas Cook	Now Lancashire Tube.
13	Darcy Lever	Croal	Site not known	*c.* 1711	James Crompton (son-in-law of Robert Crompton)	Site disappeared.
14	Lomax Bank, Little Lever	Blackshaw Brook	7514 0817	before 1783	James Sharples	Wilkinson Avenue covers the site.
15	Spring Vale, Turton Bottoms	Bradshaw Brook	738 158	*c.* 1860	James Dearden	Closed 1882.

This list shows that Crompton was a prominent family name associated with paper making in Bolton and Farnworth. The paper-making Cromptons had no direct connection with Samuel Crompton, the inventor of the mule: Crompton was, and still is, a common family name in Bolton. The family history of the Cromptons and their paper-making activities is complex. They were inter-related with other paper-making families such as the Liveseys, but two main branches can be traced. One part of the family, headed by James Crompton (*c.* 1646–1704) originally owned and developed Creams Mill at Little Lever over successive generations. The other part, headed by James's younger brother Robert Crompton (*c.* 1667–1737), was responsible for Great Lever and Farnworth paper mills.

James Crompton, who was twenty-one years older than Robert, began making paper in an old walk mill[4] on the River Irwell, which he leased from Oliver Heywood in 1677. Four generations later, after many extensions and rebuildings, the mill passed by marriage to Joseph Bealey (1783–1817), and later fell into the possession of William Broadbent (1792–1862). In 1847 Broadbent patented an improved suction box for paper-making machines. Later still the firm passed by marriage into the possession of the Hutchings family, and in 1968 the name Trinity Paper Mills was adopted.[5] The rather unusual name Creams[6] came into use in the eighteenth century, and the mill is owned today by Danisco Paper Ltd. Paper has been produced continuously on the site for well over 300 years, and Creams is probably now the oldest paper mill in south-east Lancashire, although all the existing buildings are recent. The present owners specialise in paper board and chipboard.

Cream's Paper Mill, founded in 1677 on the River Irwell. It is one of the earliest paper mills in Lancashire. *(Author's Collection)*

Robert Crompton set up Darley Hall Mill (Farnworth), on the Croal, in about 1687, and this operated until his death in 1737.[7] Robert's son Ellis (1693–1760) built a paper mill at Great Lever in 1726, and the family transferred their attention from Farnworth to this site. Around 1783 Ellis's son, another Ellis (1729–1803), built a new mill at Farnworth, believed to be on the old Darley site,[8] and this was run by his sons Robert and John. John's eldest son was Thomas Bonsor Crompton (1792–1858), who in 1820 patented the paper-drying and finishing attachment mentioned previously. In 1858 the mill passed to T.B. Crompton's nephew William Rideout, and ran until 1883, when it closed. It lay empty until reopened in 1894 by Messrs J.B. Champion & Co. as a bleachworks. The buildings were eventually demolished in the 1970s. All that remain today are a weir on the river, the lodges and Rock Hall, built for John Crompton in the year he died, and occupied subsequently by the works managers. Rock Hall is now the Croal–Irwell Valley visitor centre, located in Moses Gate County Park; the lodges there are now known as Crompton's Lodges.

A long-established paper-making firm in the Prestolee area of Farnworth is that of Robert Fletcher (Stoneclough) Ltd. Founded in 1823 by Ralph Crompton as a bleachworks, using water from the River Irwell, it changed to paper manufacture some six or so years later. It remained in the Crompton family until 1859, when the then manager Robert Fletcher bought the business and changed its name to Robert Fletcher & Sons. Robert's two sons John and James took over after their father's death, and the firm remained in the family until 1915. It still operates today under the Fletcher name as a limited company. The firm produces many varieties of paper, but is renowned for its fine tissues and cigarette papers. Many of the old buildings remain, housing modern equipment, which includes a water-treatment plant fed from the River Irwell.

Chapter 13

COAL MINING IN BOLTON & DISTRICT

oal is no longer produced in Bolton by traditional deep mining, but the industry was once an important source of male employment, particularly in Westhoughton. Documentary evidence exists that shows that local coal was won from outcrops and shallow bell pits as early as the sixteenth century. John Leland, the Tudor traveller, recorded in 1540: 'they burne at Bolton some canale, but more as cole, of which the pittes be not far off. They burne turfe also.'[1] The 1550 will of Laurence Brownlow, a landowner in Tonge, stated that his wife should 'get coles . . . as shall be sufficient for hir to burne in hir owne house all the tyme . . .'[2] And nearly two centuries later Daniel Defoe remarked in his *Tour through England and Wales* that there were plentiful supplies of cannel coal found between Wigan and Bolton.[3]

The outcrop of the Plodder seam was worked in the late seventeenth century, and the pits were drained by a sough some 1,000yds long, which discharged into a brook in Doe Hey Clough, Moses Gate.[4] Early bell-pits were often worked on a part-time domestic basis, as time became available in the farming calendar. A good example of an early bell-pit may be seen at Wayoh Fold, near the old coke ovens (see page 87), and others existed until a few years ago on the slopes of Winter Hill, close to the television mast, but these have been levelled for safety reasons. Other examples can occasionally be found elsewhere in the borough. Large-scale OS maps record shafts and pits scattered all over the area, showing that coal has been extracted at some time in nearly every part of the borough.

Coal Pit Lane on Smithills Moor originally served Holdens Colliery, which worked the Sandrock Mine (known locally as the Mountain Mine). The Ainsworths of Smithills Hall extracted coal for their bleachworks from small mines on the moors above the Hall, connected to the works by a tramway, and they built the cottages still standing on Colliers Row Road. Small overgrown spoil heaps remain, and old tramway rails are used as fencing along part of Smithills Dean Road. From 1872, under the Abandoned Mines Act, plans of underground workings have been deposited with HM Inspector of Mines, but often there are no reliable records of earlier workings. This helps to explain why reports of old shafts suddenly opening up in unexpected places appear in the local press from time to time.

In 1760 the Duke of Bridgewater began to construct his underground canal navigation system at Worsley Delph. The boats' point of exit lies outside our area, but several miles of the canal system lie beneath Bolton, a branch reaching a point below Daubhill in 1820.[5] The site of John Gilbert's underground inclined plane connecting the upper and lower canals lies approximately below the junction of Grosvenor Road and Windmill Road in Walkden, just over ¼ mile south of the Bolton borough boundary. Water for the canals was supplied from the Blackleach Reservoir. Several ventilation shafts for the underground canals were sunk in the Daubhill and Farnworth areas.

Those coal seams which lay close to the surface and were easily reached were eventually exhausted. Coal then had to be extracted using vertical shafts, which led to underground galleries spreading out to follow the various seams. In Bolton, coal seams dip between 1 in 4 and 1 in 15, from roughly the north-east down to the south-west, although there are exceptions caused by folding and faulting. The coalfield is complex, with many faults disturbing the pattern of the seams (which are called mines in Lancashire). Some seams are named after their thickness in the area where they were first worked, like the Half Yard Mine and the Five Quarters Mine. Others were named after the place where they were first worked as outcrops, like the Arley Mine, which outcropped near Arley Wood between Blackrod and Standish, or the Plodder Mine, which outcropped near Plodder Lane in Farnworth.

Two types of coal were mined in the area – cannel and bituminous, the latter in much greater tonnages. In the early nineteenth century cannel coal was much prized for the manufacture of town gas, while bituminous coal was a domestic and steam-raising fuel. The coals lay mainly in the middle and lower coal measures of the Lancashire coalfield. On the high ground to the north of Bolton the middle coal measures have been eroded away, and the seams worked were in the lower coal measures. On the lower ground south, east and west of the town the middle coal measures were the most important. In Westhoughton some thirteen seams were worked (see the list opposite). When deep mining began coal was extracted using the pillar-and-stall technique. This was an inefficient method, since a large amount of coal was left undisturbed as pillars supporting the roof of the galleries. When mechanical coal cutting was introduced from about 1870 pillar-and-stall working was replaced by the superior longwall technique, which removes all the coal.

Deep mining on a commercial basis was well established by the late eighteenth century, and the Bridgewater Trust sank many shafts between 1760 and 1860 in Dixon Green, Deane and Farnworth, to wind coal from the duke's coalfield. Two of their collieries, Buckley Lane Pit and Doe Pit, also had access to the underground canal system. Other large and powerful concerns sank many shafts in the Bolton area, including the Hulton Colliery Co., Thomas Fletcher, Andrew Knowles & Son and the Bradford Estate. As the town's industry and domestic population increased, local production was unable to cope with the demand, and coal had to be brought in from further afield, principally from the mines around Wigan. The Bolton & Leigh Railway was originally built to transport coal and cotton to Bolton.

Few surface features of Bolton's collieries remain today. All the surface buildings, headgear, winding engines, air compressor houses, sorting screens, and so on, have gone. A 1912 steel lattice headgear and engine house containing a fine steam-winding engine built by Yates & Thom of Blackburn, and in the care of the Red Rose Steam Society, may be seen at the site of Astley Green Colliery. Similar headgear, though smaller and usually built of wood, was used by Bolton collieries. Coal tips or 'rucks' may indicate the presence of a former colliery, though many of these have been landscaped or removed for redevelopment. A very large tip of waste from the pits of the former Bridgewater collieries occurs at Cutacre, Over Hulton, close to the site of Brackley Colliery.

Coke is an important by-product of coal. It was used in foundries and in blacksmiths' and farriers' forges, of which there were many in the days of the horse. Metallurgical coke was needed to produce iron, and early locomotives burned coke[6] rather than coal, to cut down the amount of smoke they produced. Early coke ovens were simple stone-lined structures, often built into the side of a hill to simplify charging and emptying, and close to bell-pits. An example of a group of early coke ovens can be seen above Wayoh Fold, Edgworth. Here coke was produced at the place where the coal was mined. In these early ovens, the gases were allowed to escape. In later years, when coal gas was produced in banks of retorts, the gases were then collected, purified and stored in gas holders. The remaining coke was then used mainly as a fuel in metallurgical processes.

PRINCIPAL COAL SEAMS WORKED IN THE BOLTON AREA

The seams are named in descending order from the surface. In different areas the same seam can be known by different names; the names listed below are those most commonly used around Bolton. Some seams are named according to their thickness where they were first worked, but seams can differ considerably in thickness and quality at different collieries.

Upper Coal Measures

Most of these measures are partly absent owing to past erosion, though the Worsley Four Foot and Pendelton Top Four Foot mines have been worked in Little Lever and eastwards.

Middle Coal Measures (where not all the seams are present in every area)

These were mainly worked in the Westhoughton, Farnworth and Blackrod areas and around Breightmet and Great Lever.

1	Rams Mine (nearest surface)	10	Trencherbone Mine
2	Lower Yard Mine	11	Cannel Mine
3	Three Yards Mine	12	King Mine
4	Four Feet Mine	13	Plodder or Ravine Mine
5	Windmill or Gingham Mine	14	Yard Mine
6	Doe Mine	15	Bone Mine
7	Five Quarters Mine	16	Cockloft or Three Quarters Mine
8	Hell Hole Mine	17	Smith Mine
9	Victoria Mine	18	Arley Mine (deepest seam)

Lower Coal Measures (mainly worked at Winter Hill, Doffcocker, Bradshaw and Affetside)

1	Darwen Cannel Mine	5	Bassey Mine
2	Upper Mountain Mine	6	Margery Mine
3	Upper Foot Mine	7	Sandrock Mine (deepest seam)
4	Lower Mountain Mine		

FAULTING

The coal seams in the Bolton area are disturbed and displaced by many faults, caused by earth movements in past geological times (see solid geology map on page 12). The principal faults in the area are:

- The Irwell Valley fault (known locally as the Pendelton fault), which runs in a north-north-westerly to south-south-easterly direction under Belmont, Smithills, Halliwell, Bolton, Moses Gate and Farnworth, and displaces the seams vertically by a considerable distance – over 2,000ft. Whenever a slight slip occurs in this fault, small earth tremors are felt in the Bolton and Farnworth areas.
- The Shipwreck fault, which runs in a west-north-westerly to east-south-easterly direction under Astley Bridge, Breightment and Little Lever.
- The Hulton Park or Padiham fault, which runs north-west to south-east from Chew Moor to below Hulton Lane Ends.
- The Eatock fault, which runs south from Westhoughton.
- The Scot Lane fault, which runs north-north-west to south-south-east from Scot Lane End to Wingates, and then continues under Westhoughton as the Church fault.

Coal mining is a dangerous occupation. The principal hazards are flooding, roof collapses and poisonous or explosive gases in the workings. In early days flooding was controlled using soughs, which drained the water by gravity, but as mines grew deeper pumping became necessary. A pump-house still stands on Tonge Moore Road, which once pumped water from Scowcroft's Pit. The ruined engine house of Pumping Pit at Aspull once contained three large vertical Bull-type steam engines.

An underground explosion of firedamp (methane gas) and coal dust occurred on 21 December 1910 in the Yard seam of no. 3 Bank Pit (Pretoria Pit) of the Hulton Colliery Co. in Westhoughton. Three hundred and forty-four men and boys died in the worst colliery disaster in Britain up to that time.[7] The pit closed in 1934, and its site is grassed over, the shafts capped. A memorial stone marks the spot. Memorabilia of the terrible event are on display in Westhoughton Public Library, with photographs of other coal-mining activities, such as pit brow lassies at the Hulton collieries. Westhoughton cemetery has a large memorial to those lost in the disaster.

Early pits were ventilated by maintaining a fire at the base of the upcast shaft. The rising hot air created a draught through the workings by drawing in fresh air through the downcast shaft. A square brick shaft which once served the ventilation furnace of Cullet Pit is preserved close to Bolton Road, Aspull. In the late nineteenth century mechanically driven fans were introduced. A large steam-driven ventilation fan of 1910 can be seen next to Trencherfield Mill on the Wigan Pier site.

Colliers have always been strong trades unionists. A union named the Friendly Society of Coal Mining was formed in Bolton as early as 1820. It lasted only seventeen months, and was smashed by the concerted action of the local coal owners.[8] In 1881 another grouping of local district unions occurred,[9] and the Lancashire and Cheshire Miners' Federation built their new headquarters in Bridgeman Place in 1914, with the name of the union in bold

In Memoriam

Sacred
to the memory of
344 MEN AND BOYS WHO LOST
THEIR LIVES BY AN EXPLOSION
AT THE PRETORIA PIT OF THE
HULTON COLLIERY Cᵒ ON
THE 21ˢᵗ DECEMBER 1910, 24
OF WHOM SLEEP UNDER THIS
MONUMENT, BEING UNIDENTIFIED
AT THE TIME OF BURIAL.
THIS MONUMENT IS ERECTED
BY PUBLIC SUBSCRIPTION, AS A
TOKEN OF SYMPATHY WITH
THE WIDOWS AND RELATIVES
OF THE VICTIMS, 171 OF WHOM
ARE BURIED IN THIS CEMETERY,
45 IN WINGATES, 20 IN DAISY
HILL, 3 IN THE CONGREGATIONAL
CHURCHYARDS, AND THE
REMAINDER IN VARIOUS
BURIAL GROUNDS.

"BE YE THEREFORE READY ALSO,
FOR THE SON OF MAN COMETH
AT AN HOUR WHEN YE THINK NOT."
Sᵗ LUKE XII. 40.

The monument to the Pretoria coal pit disaster. Three hundred and forty-four men and boys died in an underground explosion on 21 December 1910 at Pretoria Pit, Westhoughton. *(Author's Collection)*

Scot Lane No. 4 pit, Blackrod, 1950s. *(Bolton Evening News)*

lettering at roof level. Many conferences were held there, and the building became known as the Miners' Hall. It is occupied today by the Bolton and Bury Chamber of Commerce.

Many collieries had tram roads, tub ways or mineral lines, which connected them to the nearest main-line railway. Great Lever Colliery at Burnden had a short connection to the Bolton–Manchester main line. The Hulton Colliery Co. had an extensive network of sidings and mineral lines connecting several of their pits to the Bolton–Leigh main line. The Bridgewater Collieries had an extensive system of private mineral lines serving their various pits, tips and workshops, with several connections to the main-line railways. The mines of the Aberdeen and Anderton Hall Collieries connected to the Bolton–Preston line. The tracks of these mineral lines have all been lifted, but in some cases the original trackbed routes can still be traced and old bridges found – for example, the underbridge below the A6 at Greenheys, which joined the sites of Brackley Colliery and Cutacre tip. The Ladyshore Colliery at Little Lever had its own basin and wharf on the Manchester, Bolton & Bury Canal, as did Farnworth Bridge and Fogg's Collieries, near Hall Lane, Little Lever.

Coal mining in Westhoughton had reached its peak by the end of the nineteenth century. Bolton collieries shared with those nationally a lack of capital for modernisation. Inefficient working practices meant that the price of coal steadily increased, and production gradually

Victoria Colliery, Wigan Road, late 1940s. *(Bolton Evening News)*

declined. Many of the larger pits closed during the depression of the 1920s and '30s. The last pit in Westhoughton closed in 1935 due to flooding,[10] but in other parts of the borough a few still carried on. A slight revival occurred after the Second World War, but oil, natural gas and cheap foreign coal eventually killed off all the remaining pits, and deep mining ceased completely in the early 1960s. One of the last collieries to close was the small, hand-worked Victoria Colliery on Wigan Road, Hunger Hill.

In many cases the sites of former collieries have been redeveloped for housing or other purposes. Great Lever Colliery closed in 1922, and was cleared. The site became a greyhound racing track in 1927, but is now being redeveloped once again. Barton Grange garden centre occupies the site of Victoria Colliery.

Land above old mine workings can be affected by subsidence, and this can affect the structural stability of houses or other buildings, for which the National Coal Board must pay compensation. Examples of subsidence can be seen in the Over Hulton district.

Where the overburden is not too thick, coal can be won by open-cast methods, from the pillars left in old pillar-and-stall workings, or where the seam was too thin to be worked profitably in the past. The topsoil and overburden are removed and stored to one side, ready to replace after the coal has been extracted, the site landscaped and allowed to settle for a number of years. The Nicholas site near Junction 4 of the M61 motorway and the Garnet site off St Helen's Road have already been so treated. The small coal discarded in old tips can also be recovered. The Cutacre tip off Salford Road, Bolton (A6), which contains an estimated 2 million tons of coal, is under consideration for open-cast working.

Chapter 14

FERROUS &

NON-FERROUS METALS

This chapter deals with metallic materials that were once produced in the Bolton area by methods or processes no longer in use today. The end products were wrought iron, steel and lead, which were the raw materials of the engineering, machine-making and structural steel industries. The rare mineral witherite (barium carbonate), used in the pottery industry, is associated with lead.

The old method of smelting iron directly from nodules of ironstone was carried out at bloomeries.[1] These primitive methods date from the early Middle Ages, but are no longer in use. Dorning Rasbothom, writing in 1780, stated that there was a bloomery or bloomeries in the Smithills area,[2] but any traces have long since disappeared. A spring in Raveden Wood near Smithills Hall produces rust-coloured water, which indicates that iron is present, and a bloomery may possibly have been close to this site. Alternatively, the colour may be due to water draining from the old colliery workings in the area. Rust-coloured ('ochry') water occurs in several other places – for example, in the Jumbles Reservoir and on Anglezarke Moor – and nodules of ironstone occur everywhere in the coal measures, so the

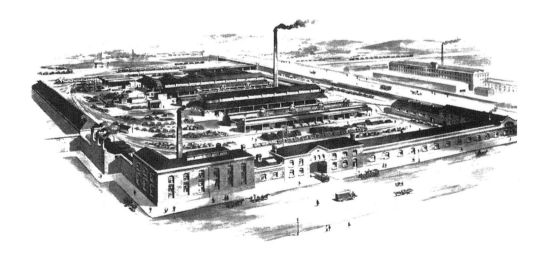

View of Atlas Forge, Bridgeman Street. *(Thomas Walmsley Ltd)*

Wrought-iron making, Atlas Forge, *c.* 1965. Puddling the iron at the melting stage.
(Bolton Museum & Art Gallery)

Shaping the red hot iron into a bar in the rolling mill, *c.* 1965. *(Bolton Museum & Art Gallery)*

discovery of possible bloomery sites in the Bolton area offers a challenge to local industrial archaeologists. The nearest known bloomery site is on Cinder Hill, Red Brook, Holcombe Hill (SD769 170), recorded in 1872.[3] After smelting, wrought-iron blooms were re-worked and refined, and then supplied to blacksmiths, nailers and other users.

In the nineteenth century wrought iron was made by the indirect or two-stage method. Cast iron from the blast furnaces was converted to wrought iron by the puddling process. The first puddling furnaces in Bolton were set up in 1866 by Thomas Walmsley (1812–90) at Atlas Forge, on the corner of Bridgeman Street and Fletcher Street. The forge was run by four generations of the same family, and when it closed in 1975 it was the only firm in Britain still making wrought iron by the hand-puddling process, and possibly the only one in the world. By this date the market for wrought iron had effectively disappeared, being replaced by cheap mild steel produced by the Bessemer and open-hearth processes. The forge contained coal-fired (later oil-fired) reverberatory puddling furnaces, steam-driven shingling hammers,[4] and rolling mills. A siding from the adjacent LNWR brought in coal, pig iron and other supplies. The company made various grades of wrought-iron bars, rounds, flats, bridge rails, and so on, some of which were exported as far as New Zealand.[5] At its peak the forge employed up to 300 men. In its declining years wrought iron was produced by re-working scrap, especially axles from old railway wagons. After closure the site was cleared for housing, but a shingling hammer made by Nasmyth was presented by the firm in 1981 to Bolton University, and erected outside the main building. A complete set of furnaces, hammer and steam-driven rolls was sent to Blists Hill Open Air Museum in 1983, where the puddling process is demonstrated from time to time. The concrete effigy of Atlas supporting the world, which once adorned the forge as its trademark, was rescued, restored and re-sited in 1989 at the entrance to the subway under St Peter's Way at Kay Street.

In 1835 the firm of Rushton & Eckersley, Iron Founders, took over an existing small forge on Blackhorse Street. In 1860 the firm changed hands and became the Bolton Iron & Steel Co. In 1882 the adjoining Union Foundry of Rothwell & Co. was absorbed, making the company one of the largest in the country. The works covered a large area, bounded by Moor Lane, Blackhorse Street, New Street and Railway Street. The last-named street has disappeared under later developments. A branch ran from the LNWR Bolton–Kenyon line through the works to the railway company's Deansgate goods warehouse (now demolished), behind the present White Lion pub. Sidings from the branch enabled coal, pig iron, limestone and other raw materials to be brought in, and finished products dispatched to customers by rail. A system of internal tracks allowed materials to be moved within the works itself.

In 1906 the works were taken over by Henry Bessemer & Co. of Sheffield,[6] and became known as Bessemer's Foundry. From around 1900 the Siemens-Martin open-hearth process of making steel began to supersede the Bessemer process. This led to a reduced demand for the foundry's steel, and by 1924 the works had closed and the entire plant and railway sidings sold to another Sheffield firm, Thomas Ward.[7] The site was cleared by early 1927, and in 1930 the bus station was transferred from Victoria Square to part of the site. In 1932 the wholesale and retail markets were opened on another part of the site. The closure of Bessemer's Foundry marked the end of heavy engineering in Bolton.

The works was well equipped for manufacturing articles in wrought iron and Bessemer and Siemens steel, having puddling furnaces, steam hammers, rolling mills, Bessemer

Aerial view of Moor Lane area, *c*. 1928. In the centre is the cleared site of the former Bessemer Foundry, makers of iron and steel. In 1930 the bus station was transferred to it from Victoria Square, and two years later the wholesale retail markets arrived. *(Bolton Museum & Art Gallery)*

converters, hydraulic presses, and so on. Its products included steel rails for trams and railways, rolled steel joists and related sections, steel plates of various thicknesses, forged steel items and iron castings, for the engineering, construction and transport industries.

Veins of the ore galena (lead sulphide) often occur in limestone, and were discovered in about 1692 at Limestone Clough on Anglezarke Moor, north-west of Bolton. Over the years the veins were worked intermittently, and always unprofitably, up to 1837, the last operator being John Thompson of Wigan. Compared with other Pennine lead mines, these were of only minor importance. The open shafts were filled in around 1930 by unemployed men from Chorley,[8] but in 1982–3 some of the surface remains were excavated and consolidated by the British Trust for Conservation Volunteers. The excavations were

Early eighteenth-century bell pits on Anglezarke Moor. In the centre are three pits following the line of a lead vein. *(Author's Collection)*

fenced off, and interpretation boards set up at various points in the clough. Other traces of lead-mining activity occur nearby at Stronstrey Bank, White Coppice, and near the ruined farm of Drinkwaters in the valley of the Dean Black Brook.

The visible remains in Limestone Clough (also called Lead Mines Valley) include spoil heaps, bell-pits, exits from drainage soughs, a pumping shaft, wheel pit and slime pit. The wheel pit once had a wooden waterwheel of about 18ft diameter, which operated flat rods and T-bobs to drive pumps down the shaft, raising water from the underground workings. The wheel was supplied by water from a spring, via a wooden launder supported on stone pillars. Some of the pillars have been reconstructed. The ore was probably separated by hand from the unwanted material on dressing floors nearby, but little trace of these remains, apart from the slime pit, which was used to trap the smallest particles of lead ore. The ore was probably smelted at White Coppice, about $2\frac{1}{2}$ miles away, but the site of the smelter is unknown. An old plan shows that the principal veins of lead run in a roughly north-easterly direction. They had names such as Sun Vein, String Vein and South Level. Other veins crossed these, running in a north-westerly direction. The lead produced was probably used for roofing, plumbing items, musket balls, pellets for shotguns and pottery glazes.

Conservation volunteers at Anglezarke lead mine, c. 1982. *(Bolton Evening News)*

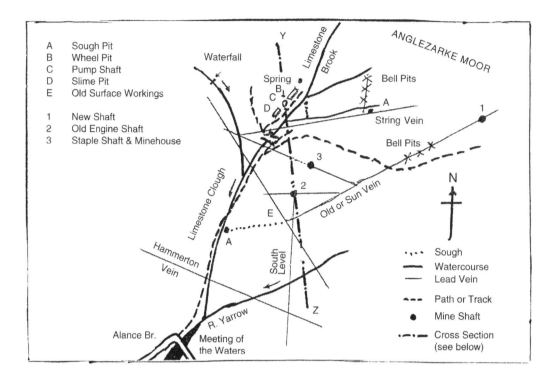

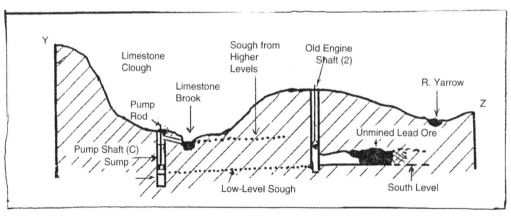

Sketch plans of Anglezarke lead mine. *(Author's Collection)*

Dr William Withering discovered a new mineral in the Anglezarke area, which he reported in 1783. He called it 'terra ponderosa aereata', but it is now known as witherite (barium carbonate). James Watt Jnr visited the mines and reported on them to the Manchester Literary & Philosophical Society. The eighteenth-century miners had no use for witherite, and threw it on the dumps, but Josiah Wedgwood (1730–95) secretly began to use it as a glaze for his pottery. Some German potters heard of this, and obtained supplies from a Rivington farmer who covertly gathered pieces of witherite from the spoil heaps.[9] Samples of galena, witherite and barite (barium sulphate) can still be found on the old spoil heaps, but the best samples can be seen in Bolton Museum.

Chapter 15

WORKERS' HOUSES

This chapter deals with industrial housing – the accommodation for workers at mills and factories, mines and quarries, as distinct from the cottages where domestic workers lived, such as weavers and nailers, which was covered in chapter 4.

The first cotton mills were built in what at the time were rural areas, where streams and rivers were available to drive waterwheels, but a local population from which workers could be drawn was largely absent. Public transport to carry town-based workers to and from the mills did not exist at this time, and so several mill and factory owners built cottages close to their enterprise to attract labour away from the town, or made land available for building, thus creating industrial communities or villages. Bolton has the remnants of four early villages dating from the early nineteenth century, and one late Victorian community.

The Ashworth family[1] built two cotton mills north of the town – New Eagley Mill in 1802/3 and Egerton Mill in 1829, both on the Eagley Brook. They began building cottages at Bank Top in about 1820 to house part of their New Eagley Mill labour force. By 1867 there were seventy-one terraced two-storey cottages rented out to their workers, a school, a library and newsroom, and two shops, all constructed of local stone. The cottages varied from two-up, two-down to three- and four-bedroom dwellings, each with a separate outside lavatory in a high-walled private backyard, with gas for lighting piped from the mill's gasholder.[2] The cottages were generally superior to those built at that time by speculative builders for town-based mill workers. A contemporary observer writing in 1842 said of them: 'they are good substantial stone buildings, roomy, well drained, well lighted, well watered and well aired, having one door in front and another at the back . . . .'.[3] Several of these cottages still stand at Bank Top, though modernised, as in Park Row. School Street was built for workmen, and Vale View for foremen at the factory.

To house about three-quarters of their workers at Egerton Mill,[4] the Ashworths built a new village, which by 1844 had almost 100 stone-built cottages, a library and a newsroom, all on similar lines to Bank Top. Modernised examples of the cottages can be seen today in the vicinity of the mill.

Many workers at Wallsuches Bleachworks were originally housed in an area in Horwich lying to the south of Church Street, on land provided in 1802 by Joseph Ridgway (1765–1842), proprietor of the bleachworks. A terminating building society deed was drawn up between Ridgway and some of his workers to help them build their own houses on the land.[5] This resulted in terraced houses in Nelson Street, Duncan Street and other adjoining streets, originally totalling some 150 cottages in all. The whole village was designated a conservation area in 1975, and is known locally as the club houses. Club houses were also built in other parts of Bolton, such as in Halliwell Road, and in other parts of Lancashire, from the late eighteenth century. The scheme operated in this way. A group of workers would join together to form a club or society, with the intention of building for themselves an agreed number of houses. Regular payments were made into a central fund, and when sufficient money had accumulated, either one or a few houses were built. A lottery was then held and the winner(s) moved in. Everyone continued paying until another house or houses could be built and occupied by the winner(s) of a new lottery. This continued until every member of the club had been housed, after which the club was dissolved. On terraced houses built by this method a vertical joint in the masonry or brickwork marks where each group of houses was built, and this can be seen on the Horwich club houses, confirmed by datestones. The Horwich club houses are two-storey, stone-built, and many have cellars. Some of the cellars were used for handloom weaving, but most of the original owner-occupiers worked as bleachers, crofters, or in other occupations at the bleachworks. Many of these houses still exist, but have often been modernised or altered. It has been suggested that they were possibly originally of back-to-back construction.

Club houses can be identified if the houses either side of the vertical lines are of the same design or style. If the houses are different styles (with different windows, door size, and so on), this may be because the row was extended by a different builder at a different date.

Barrow Bridge industrial village was built in the years 1835–7 by Robert Gardner (1780–1866) and his partner Thomas Bazley (1798–1885), proprietors of Dean Mill, Barrow Bridge. The village comprised five rows of two-storey back-to-back stone cottages, in parallel streets named First Street through to Fifth Street, all leading off Bazley Street.

Club houses, Horwich. Handloom weaving took place in the cellars reached from inside the house. *(Author's Collection)*

A communal wash-house was built at the west end of each row, and all the dwellings had running water from a nearby reservoir, and domestic gas lighting and street lighting piped from the mill gasholder. This type of accommodation was for the ordinary workers. In addition, some detached and semi-detached houses were built along one side of Barrow Bridge Road for the manager and foremen. A truck shop was built, facing the foremen's houses. In 1846 a school, library and newsroom, known as the Institute, were built in Bazley Street.[6] By 1877, when the mill closed, there were seventy-six cottages, the shop and the manager's house,[7] but gradually, as the mill lay empty, the families moved away and the buildings became derelict, earning in time the title of the 'Deserted Village'.[8] By the middle of the twentieth century the village began to be inhabited again, and the old back-to-back cottages have been turned into modernised dwellings. The Grade II listed Institute has been converted into flats and named Barrowdene House, and the old truck shop is now a private residence. The village has been designated a conservation area.

The fourth nineteenth-century industrial community is that built by the Chadwicks in 1831–68 for their Eagley Mills. In addition to cottages for the workers, a fire station, shops, a school, and an ornamental park were provided.

The Lancashire & Yorkshire Railway Co. built a late-Victorian industrial community next to their new engineering works, on the south side of Chorley New Road, Horwich. The works was built from 1884 to 1886, and at the same time twelve streets of brick two-storey terraced houses with slate roofs were erected for their employees. Many skilled men brought their families to Horwich from the L. & Y. works at Miles Platting, Manchester, soon after the new works started up. The streets were named after famous engineers, and the area became known locally as Railway Terraces. Some years later another dozen or so streets bearing engineers' names were built facing the original streets, but on the northern side of Chorley New Road. These later streets had semi-detached houses. A number of the original terraces have survived. In 1888 a Mechanics' Institute was built, and in 1895 a small cottage hospital was built to serve both the railway community and the surrounding district. The Mechanics' Institute was demolished in 1976 and the latter remains in different use, but has cottage hospital still inscribed on it.

Cottages in small, isolated groups were built for colliers and for quarry workers, and examples can still be found. Colliers' Row and New Colliers' Row cottages on Colliers' Row Road, above Smithills, are good examples. Colliers' Row comprises a row of seven late-eighteenth-century cottages with stone slab roofs. About $^{1}/_{4}$ mile east is New Colliers' Row, consisting of four similar cottages, but with slate roofs, built almost a century later. The change in roof material probably reflects the use of Welsh slate, which became more readily available as the railway system developed. Near the latter is a small school, dated 1885, now a private residence. These cottages and school were built by the Ainsworth family of Smithills Hall to house the colliers working their coal mines on Smithills Moor. Small groups of miners' cottages can still be seen in the Westhoughton district – for example at Hart Common, and near the railway station. Quarry workers' cottages can be found at Wallsuches, and along Georges Lane, Horwich, and at Round Barn Quarry, above Wayoh Fold, Edgworth.

Steam-driven mills on the fringes of the town were built in the mid-nineteenth century, and rows of terraced houses were built close to the mills, so that mill employees could walk to work. Horse-drawn trams were not available until the late 1870s. The houses

An aerial view of Stanley Mill and houses. This 1920s view shows the mill surrounded by rows of terraced workers' houses and is typical of a mill community once common in Bolton. In the area are a church, chapel, two schools, probably many corner shops and pubs, all catering for the needs of the community, nearly all of whom worked in the mill. The area is much altered today; the mill was demolished in 1974. *(Bolton Museum & Art Gallery)*

were usually red brick, built either by speculative builders and rented out, or in some cases financed by the mill company. There were also instances where tradesmen such as shopkeepers and butchers with spare cash built a few houses as an investment and for rent income. The worst type of houses were the back-to-backs: cheap, poorly constructed and crowded together for maximum profit. Some houses had cellar dwellings reached by separate entrance steps, which ran down from the street. Courts containing more houses were sometimes built behind the terraces, often reached by a tunnel passageway left in the front row or by a narrow alleyway from the street. A few modernised courts have survived, such as Mort Court, off Halliwell Road. Housing like this led to overcrowding under insanitary conditions, and the building of back-to-back houses was prohibited by an Act in 1844. Some of these houses survived as late as the 1950s, but all have now been demolished.

When first built, the houses surrounding the mills were all occupied by families employed at the mills: father, mother, and grown-up sons and daughters. An investigation of the industrial working classes by the *Morning Chronicle* newspaper in 1849 reported on certain Bolton mills: 'that it is a condition that the spinner shall live in a house belonging to the employer. In the workpeople's own phraseology "a key goes to each set of mules". . . .'[9]

Many streets of houses once occupied by mill workers survive in various parts of the town, particularly where there were large mills. The houses in terraced rows range from the early nineteenth century to the first decade or two of the twentieth, after which date cotton manufacture in Bolton began to decline. The changes in house construction and design over the period can be studied by the observant industrial archaeologist. The earliest types that remain are usually two-up, two-down, entered directly from the street pavement, with a small backyard enclosed by a high wall with a gate leading into a back access street. The backyard would originally have had a brick privy fitted with an earth closet. The closet would have been replaced later by a flushing WC, when waterborne sewerage was installed. The backyard also included a coal store, as coal was the only fuel available for cooking, and for room and water heating. In some houses the coal was stored in a cellar, and the houses were lit by town gas. There was no bathroom. Externally, the cheaper houses were plain, with minimum or no decoration, brick walls, stone sills and lintels, and Welsh slate roofs. The small privy building may still remain in some backyards, but changed to other uses when an internal lavatory was installed.

Writing of workers' houses in the nineteenth century, Allen Clarke (1863–1935) said:

they are mostly small four-roomed (two above, two below) cottages rents varying from 3s 6d to 5s 6d. They have no baths as a rule. Each house is one of a long row, like a barracks, divided into so many equal portions. . . . The houses have generally scant backyard space, the jerry builder wishes to squeeze as much property on the land as possible, and tries to cheat the building and sanitary authorities as much as he can.[10]

Later demands for more privacy and improved living conditions resulted in better designs of industrial housing. First came the internal lobby or narrow entrance hall, a minuscule front garden to keep passers-by at a distance from the front windows, and inside lavatory and bathroom. Externally, some ornamentation was indulged in by the builder, such as moulded dentils supporting the gutters, the use of coloured bricks to form string courses and other patterns, tiny iron balustrades on window sills, bay windows, open-back gardens instead of walled backyards, and so on.

Each builder had his own design or style of house. The houses on both sides of some streets were built at the same time by the same builder, giving a uniform appearance to the terraces. There are examples where one builder built one side of the street and a different builder the other, resulting in different house styles in the same street. Sometimes a larger house was built at the end of each terraced row or in the middle, usually occupied by a foreman or overseer who could afford the higher rent. Waldeck Street, off Chorley Old Road, Halliwell, is a good example of different styles within the same street.

Model houses financed by Dr Chadwick. *(Author's Collection)*

In the 1850s workers' housing in Bolton was most unsatisfactory, particularly that in the inner town districts, where overcrowding was endemic. A chlolera outbreak occurred in 1848, causing great concern in the medical profession. Unhealthy cellars were still being occupied. Many Irish immigrants, escaping from the Potato Famine of 1846, were living in slum conditions around the top end of Newport Street and in Great Moor Street, an area which became known as Irish Town. Determined efforts were made by the authorities to improve and control housing conditions by introducing better building regulations and sanitation. Dr Samuel Chadwick (1809–76), a well-known benefactor of Bolton, set the example by establishing a charitable trust to 'erect model dwellings for workpeople now condemned to live in cellars'. He had built in 1869/70 some terraced houses in Peabody Street, Great Lever, and in Halstead Street in the Haulgh, which for the time were of a greatly advanced design. The houses have in recent years been restored and modernised, and may still be seen today.

Eventually local councils were permitted to build houses to much better standards for the working classes. Following the Housing and Town Planning Act of 1909, Bolton Corporation built its first Council Housing Estate at Platt Hill in 1919/20, when 237 dwellings for rent were erected. Other estates followed, and by 1953 some 8,490 houses had been built in various parts of the town.[11] By then semi-detached houses usually predominated, backyards had been replaced by rear gardens, and overcrowding was controlled by the council.

Chapter 16

TRACKS & TURNPIKES

It is essential for the economy of any town to be able to maintain contact with other places and people. Over the centuries paths and tracks across the open country between adjoining towns were laid down by the passage of countless feet and hooves; many of these paths still exist and can be walked over today. With the passage of time some have developed into roads, while others have fallen into disuse. Some have disappeared without trace.

The earliest trackway in the Bolton area is probably that across the moors at Winter Hill. Dating from the fourteenth century, it was used by the monks of the Knights Hospitallers, who had a hospice in the Hill Top district of Halliwell. They also held land near Anglezarke, where it is thought they owned mines.[1] Whether these were lead or coal mines is uncertain, but the monks used a track along a ridge to and from the mines and Hill Top. The ridge is marked as Spitlers Edge on OS maps.

From the seventeenth century onwards cattle were driven south from areas north of the Ribble, where they were bred, to supply the needs of the growing populations of south Lancashire and Manchester. Drovers' roads across the moors above Bolton are shown on early maps,[2] but traces of them on the ground have long since disappeared. The trade flourished in the eighteenth century, but died out with the coming of railway, when cattle travelled in trucks rather than on hoof to the slaughter houses.

What roads existed in the seventeenth and eighteenth centuries were poorly made and badly maintained. In his journal John Wesley grumbled about the 'miserable roads between Bolton and Blackburn' in 1781, and again in 1788. In winter roads were often impassable to wheeled traffic, and not much better in the summer, so pack horses and Galloway ponies were used for carrying all kinds of loads. Since they were not pulling carts behind them, there was no need to try to follow the bad roads, and a network of tracks developed across open country and moorland. Many of these old pathways may still be traced today. The tracks were also used by pedlars travelling on foot, visiting outlying farms and hamlets to sell their wares. It was while walking on the track over Winter Hill in a thick mist in 1838 that a young pedlar or packman was shot dead and robbed. Many years afterwards an iron memorial called Scotchman's Stump was set up near the spot where the unsolved murder took place.

There are physical remains of some packhorse routes in and around Bolton. Where a watercourse had to be crossed, there was either a ford or a narrow stone packhorse bridge over which the loaded ponies passed in a line. The side walls of a packhorse bridge were originally low, so that they did not obstruct the panniers hanging down each side of the pony. When the days of the packhorses were over, the bridge walls were made higher, or railings were added for the safety of later users. An old ford across the Dean Brook at Barrow Bridge was once used by packhorses coming down Longshaw Ford Road, and continuing on the other side up a track across what is now Old Links golf course and on towards Wigan.

Three packhorse bridges remain in the Bolton area. All are Grade II listed structures, and the Old Ringley bridge is also a scheduled ancient monument. They are:

- Turton Bottoms bridge, over the Bradshaw Brook. Built in about 1691, it is a single stone arch, carrying the Affetside to Chapeltown track. Also known locally as Saddle Bridge.
- Prestolee bridge, over the River Irwell. Built in the late eighteenth century, with three arches, it carried a track from Radcliffe to Farnworth.
- Old Ringley bridge also over the River Irwell. It was built in 1677 to replace an earlier wooden bridge. It has three arches and carried an important track from Yorkshire to Manchester.

The Packhorse Inn at Affetside, built in about 1443, was frequented by jaggers (the men in charge of packhorse trains), who used the route of the old Roman road[3] past the inn on their way from Preston to Manchester, via Radcliffe. Rivington village lay on a packhorse route and near the green is a half-hidden old horse drinking trough fed from a spring. There were also horse troughs scattered along packhorse tracks, but most have disappeared today. Where the land was marshy, large flat stones were laid in a line forming a raised causeway for packhorses to cross the soft ground safely. Longcauseway in Farnworth was once a marshy stretch of packway, and the name survives showing its original form.

Packhorse bridge, Kearsley. *(Author's Collection)*

In addition to packways used for transporting all kinds of commodities, there are tracks which were made specifically for carrying one type of load. Three examples are:

- The track from Newfields Brickworks (also called Burnt Edge Colliery and now only a ruin) on Smithills Moor to Walker Fold Road, to bring coal and fire bricks from the mine (the mine worked a seam of coal with a good quality fireclay lying below it; both were extracted and used).
- The track from Holden's Colliery down to Coalpit Road, past the remains of the shooting lodge (this was the site of the mass trespass of the 1890s).
- The track from Anglezarke Mine in the valley of Limestone Brook, joining the lane at the bridge over the Yarrow Reservoir. This was used for taking dressed lead ore to a smelter believed to be situated in White Coppice.

By the middle of the eighteenth century the volume and weight of goods requiring transport were greater than could be handled by packhorses. Carts and wagons could carry far greater loads if the roads could be improved. To fund the cost of these improvements, turnpikes were introduced, administered by trustees who were usually an association of local landowners and industrialists. An Act of Parliament was needed before turnpike users could be charged a toll to pass along the road under the control of the Trust. A Turnpike Act usually lasted twenty-one years, and could be renewed for further terms. To prevent unauthorised use, a horizontal spiked bar (the pike) was set up across each entrance to the road, and tolls were collected at it before the toll keeper opened (i.e. turned) the barrier to permit entrance. Later, gates replaced bars. The money collected was used to maintain the road and pay the toll keepers. Turnpiked roads reduced transport costs, journey times were cut, and year-round travel became possible. In time, turnpikes became the major roads in Britain. Packhorse travel gradually declined as turnpikes spread across the country; it survived longer in remote areas, but eventually disappeared completely.

The following list gives the dates of the major turnpikes in and around Bolton and the routes of the turnpikes today. In some cases additional Acts were obtained to increase the powers of the original Act, or for adding extensions or branches, which are also shown.

Turnpikes in and around Bolton

No.	Name of Turnpike Trust	Date	Present-day Route	Later Acts
1.	Salford to Bolton & Duxbury (also known as Westhoughton Turnpike)	1753	Manchester Road (WK) through to Chorley Road (AD) A6	
2.	Bolton to Leigh	1762	St Helen's Road (A579) to Newbrook Road (A5979)	1788
3.	Bolton to Nightingales (also known as Doffcocker Turnpike)	1763	Chorley Old Road (BN) B6226, Lee Lane (HO), Bolton Road (AN) A673	1784–5, 1805, 1835, 1854, 1855

continued overleaf

4.	Bolton to Edenfield Chapel	1797	Tonge Moor Road (BN)	1809, 1830,
			Bradshaw Road (BN) A676	1860, 1861
5.	Bolton to Blackburn	1797	Blackburn Road (BN) A666	1810, 1830,
				1851, 1861, 1862
6.	Bolton to Westhoughton	1800	Deane Road (A676) Wigan Road	1821
			(BN) A676/A58 Bolton Road	
			(WN) B5235	
7.	Sharples to Hoghton	1801	Belmont Road (BN) A675	1823, 1852, 1874
8.	Moses Gate to Irlams	1804	Bolton Road (FN) A6053	1825
	i' th' Height		Market Street (FN) A6053	
9.	Westhoughton to	1817	Manchester Road (WN) A6,	1826, 1854
	Duxbury Stocks		Manchester Road (BL) B5408	
10.	Bolton to Bury	1821	Bury Road (BN) A58	1851, 1852
11.	Bolton to Manchester	1821	Manchester Road (BN) B6536,	1851
			Market Street (FN) A6053,	
			Bolton Road (FN) A666	
12.	Bolton to Horwich	1824	Chorley New Road (BN) A673	
13.	Westhoughton to Ince	1825	Wigan Road (WN) A58	
14.	Westhoughton to Salford	1826	Manchester Road (WN)	
	(also known as the Hulton		A6, Salford Road (OH) A6	
	Turnpike)			
15.	Bolton to St Helen's	1829	Derby Street (BN) A579,	1860, 1864
			St Helen's Road (BN) A579,	
			Newbrook Road (OH) A579	
16.	Bolton to Radcliffe	1836	Ainsworth Road (BN) B6292	

AD = Adlington, AN = Anderton, BL = Blackrod, BN = Bolton, FN = Farnworth,
HO = Horwich, KE = Kearsley, OH = Over Hulton, WK = Walkden, WN = Westhoughton

Most turnpikes ran at a loss. In 1864 a Select Committee of the House of Commons recommended that turnpikes should be wound up as soon as was reasonably possible. Competition from railways reduced the amount of traffic using them. For example, tolls collected on the Bolton to Blackburn turnpike in 1846 were £3,998 but by 1849 had fallen to £1,185, as the Bolton to Blackburn Railway had opened in 1847.[4] The last turnpike toll house to be closed in Bolton was at Daubhill, in 1879.

Turnpike Trusts often controlled several roads in an area, not merely the main road, as branches from it were sometimes included. An example is the Bolton to Nightingales Turnpike Trust (see map opposite). Roads entering the system that were not turnpiked were controlled by side bars or gates. Toll houses were designed to give a good view of the road in each direction, and a board displaying the scale of charges was prominently displayed on an outside wall. Some old toll houses still exist in and around Bolton. Two examples are Doffcocker Toll House, 765 Chorley Old Road, on the Bolton to Nightingales turnpike (1763 Act) and Halliwell Toll House, 259 Halliwell Road, on the same turnpike (extension Act of 1805).

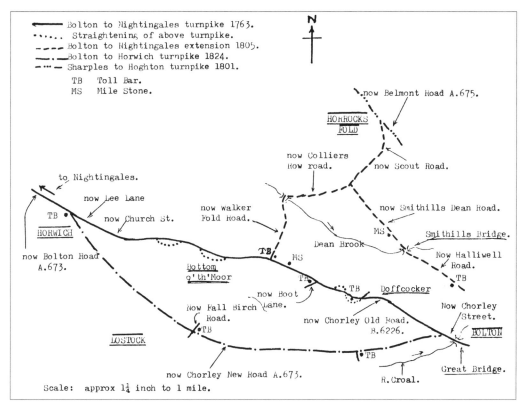

A sketch plan of Bolton to Horwich turnpikes. *(Author's Collection)*

Turnpike toll house, Doffcocker. In the centre is the old toll house of the Bolton to Nightingales turnpike. *(Author's Collection)*

Doffcocker Toll House was built in March 1785, but is actually the second one at this place. Tolls were first collected at a cottage (now demolished) near Brook Place, where a surviving stretch of the turnpike still exists. This length, paved with the original stone setts, runs behind the present toll house from the Hope & Anchor pub, turns right and crosses the present Chorley Old Road to become Caley Street, and joins New Church Road before turning left to rejoin Chorley Old Road.[5] An old cast-iron weighbridge platform by Rothwell, Hick & Rothwell (1825–33) lies close to the original route, and was probably used by the Doffcocker Colliery, which had several shafts in the vicinity. In 1784 this dog-leg was eliminated by straightening the turnpike, and the new toll house was built.[6] A new weighbridge was also installed. When the Trust was abolished in 1877 the toll house was sold by public auction,[7] the weighbridge was taken by a coal merchant[8] and local farmers bought the gates. A commemorative blue plaque was later placed on the wall of the toll house by the Civic Trust.

The sites for some former toll houses or side bars are remembered in the names of buildings or roads. Examples include Toll Bar Inn, 2 Chorley New Road, Horwich; Bar Lane (off Blackburn Road), Sharples; and Nab Gate Hotel, 1 Arthur Lane, Harwood. Old milestones provide other relics of the turnpike age, and a score or more of these can still be found in and around Bolton. The Trusts had a statutory obligation to install these, so that the correct toll could be levied. After the abolition of turnpikes the roads were taken over by local authorities, who became responsible for their upkeep and improvement.

Chapter 17

ROAD TRANSPORT IN THE NINETEENTH & EARLY TWENTIETH CENTURIES

Until electric traction by tramcars was introduced in 1899 public transport in Bolton relied on the horse for motive power, as did commercial traffic and private transport. Horse-drawn wagons or carts carried the materials for building and equipping nineteenth-century mills and factories, and collected raw cotton from the canal wharf – or, after 1830, from the railway warehouses. The finished goods were dispatched in the same way. The working population walked to and from work, since they lived close to the mills, mines and factories. Later in the century those who lived further away used horse-drawn buses, when these became available. The well-to-do, the gentry and professional people had their own gigs or carriages for getting about, while the cab ranks in the town centre provided a service for those without their own transport who could afford it.

Some relics of the old horse days may still be seen. Many former mill owners' or master bleachers' houses still have old stables, now converted to other uses. A fine example is the former stables of Smithills Hall, now the Coaching House restaurant. In the entrance yard a horse drinking trough has been re-sited, typical of the many which were once dotted around the town and countryside.

Stagecoaches travelling along the turnpikes provided public transport over longer distances, until the developing railway system drove them out of business, by the mid-nineteenth century. Several town centre inns and hotels were originally connected with the coaching trade. The Swan Hotel in Bradshawgate was a well-known coaching inn in 1824.[1] Coaches left there three days a week for the Manchester Cotton Exchange, and services to York and Carlisle were run on a regular basis. The Man & Scythe in Churchgate was another starting point for coaches for Rochdale, Halifax and Leeds. When the Bolton to Horwich turnpike (Chorley New Road) opened for traffic on 3 October 1829, the first stagecoaches to use it were the 'Invincible' and the 'New Times' coming out of Bolton. Later in the same morning came the 'North Star' from Kendal, heading for the Ship Inn in Bradshawgate.[2] The restored 'North Star' stagecoach is displayed in the entrance yard of the Smithills Coaching House Restaurant. The Red Lion at Hulton Lane Ends was an important stopping point for Royal Mail coaches on the London to Carlisle route (the A6).

Blackburn to Bolton stage coach. *(Author's Collection)*

Stagecoaches carried parcels as well as passengers, but heavy goods were carried by horse-drawn stage wagons. Often based at a pub, regular services were maintained by carriers such as John Smith to Preston, and John Hargreaves to Scotland.[3] The names of some pubs are reminders of this traffic – for example, the Jolly Wagoner on Deane Road (the old Bolton to Westhoughton turnpike), and the Carters Arms on Belmont Road (the old Sharples to Houghton turnpike).

To serve the transport industry, there were many carriage builders, wheelwrights, farriers, and so on. Samuel Gordon, carriage builder of the 1820s, was the founder of the well-known garage and motor dealership that still carries the same name. Henry Julian of Knowsley Street was still making horse carriages in 1878, when he won an award at the Paris Exhibition for a phaeton carriage.

As the town grew in size a need arose for public transport to and from outlying districts, and later on for a town centre system. Private enterprise initially provided for the first need, and Bolton Corporation provided for the second.[4] Edmund Holden started up a horse-drawn bus service in the 1870s using the ordinary roads. Belmont, Darcy Lever, Egerton, Hawkshaw, Horwich and Little Hulton were destinations for his buses, which were drawn by four-horse and five-horse teams, according to the distance and terrain involved.

Horse-drawn bus at Bradshaw, *c.* 1875. *(Bolton Evening News)*

In 1879/80 the Corporation laid the first stretches of metal tracks in the streets, using a gauge of 4ft 8½in (the same as the railways).[5] At that time they were not allowed by law to operate the system themselves, so they leased it to Holden, who ran horse-drawn trams, starting in September 1880. Less effort was needed to pull the trams along the smooth rails, and so fewer horses were required. Double-deck trams were pulled by three horses, and a single-deck tram needed only two. The trams were kept and the horses stabled in a depot at Shifnall Street, near the town centre.

Anticipating the change to electricity, more generators were added to the 1894 Spa Road lighting station, and in 1899 Mather & Platt 550V DC dynamos driven by Musgrave steam engines were installed. Holden's widow sold 48 trams and 330 horses to the Corporation in the same year, and the Shiffnall Street depot was converted to house electric trams. Hick Hargreaves supplied an overhead travelling crane to the depot. Electric trams using the overhead wire system first started running from Shifnall Street to Bradshaw Brow in December 1899. The last horse tram ran in January 1900.

The electric tram system was extended over the following years to cover Bolton and Farnworth, and to reach several destinations outside the borough boundary. In 1902 some main roads entering the town were widened to accommodate twin tram tracks, and a few

Bolton electric tramcar of 1901. *(Bolton Evening News)*

years later tram sheds were built in Horwich, Hulton Lane, Farnworth, and in Bridgeman Street. A generating station was also built in Albert Road, Farnworth. Connections with other surrounding authorities were made to allow through-running to places such as Bury and Swinton. The possibility of bringing raw cotton from Liverpool by trams running over five independent but connected systems was investigated, but this never materialised.[6]

By the beginning of the twentieth century the internal combustion engine was competing with electric traction. Bolton had experimented with a Darracq-Serpollet double-decker steam-driven bus (reg. BN 229) in 1907, but had abandoned it as unsuitable. A 12hp Stirling petrol bus (reg. BN 140) had been tried out earlier, in 1903/4, followed by others, including a Commer bus in 1908–11. But these also proved unsuitable, so electric trams continued in use for many years. In fact the first permanent internal-combustion-engined bus service did not commence until December 1923, so for many years the Corporation ran both electric trams and motor buses. The last electric tram ran in March 1947, on the same route as the first one had forty-eight years earlier. Tram tracks and poles were pulled up as each service ceased operating, leaving motor buses with their better mobility to provide for the travelling needs of the public. A bus garage was opened in Crook Street in 1929.

In addition to Bolton Corporation running buses, there were a few private operators, such as Ribble Motor Services of Preston, and John Robert Tognarelli of Manchester Road. The latter ran a bus service from 1916 to 1929 from Bolton to Manchester, and charabancs as far afield as Scotland and London, on occasion. Electric traction put in a reappearance in the

Farnworth electricity station. *(A. Wolstenholme)*

1930s, when the Farnworth to Atherton route was taken over by trolley buses in 1931, and Bolton to Leigh in 1933. These ran until 1958. Some relics of tram days can still be found. No horse buses have survived, but Bolton Corporation's double-deck electric tram no. 66 of 1901 was restored in Bolton, and runs today on Blackpool's promenade.

The first private motor car to be registered in Bolton (reg. BN 1) was a 15hp Panhard-Levassor. That was in November 1903, the owner being Joseph Magee, a brewer, who lived at Markland Hill. In those early days of motoring petrol was bought in 2-gallon cans, and there were only a few places licensed to store it. However, as the number of vehicles increased, garages began springing up in the town to serve the new form of transport. By the outbreak of the First World War there were several garages providing car sales, repairs and petrol to the pioneer motorists. Among these pioneers were Gordons, who were one of the first UK agents for Ford, and Parkside Motors, both of whom remain in business.

The war caused a temporary halt in car manufacture, but after things returned to normal the number of cars in Bolton began to increase. At a traffic census taken in 1922, 2,715 cars were counted in twelve hours, using the main roads out of Bolton.[7] In the 1920s and early 1930s a few cars of local manufacture, the Merrall-Brown and the MEB, appeared for a short while on Bolton roads.

The Merrall-Brown was a three-wheeler with an 8hp JAP petrol engine, made by the brothers Louis and Bernard Merrall-Brown in their Premier Motor Works, St George's Road, between 1919 and 1921. Only about twenty-seven were made with a novel transmission, which proved to be unsuccessful.[8] The Premier Motor Works building is now occupied by Hardmans & McManus Funeral Service. The MEB was another three-wheeler with a JAP engine, made by Maurice Edwards (1877–1971) between 1928 and the mid-1930s. This car was much more successful, and in August 1928 broke the existing world speed record in France for the 500cc class. As far as is known, no example of the car has survived, but some Bolton car enthusiasts are building a replica.

Another late nineteenth- and early twentieth-century form of transport that must not be overlooked is the humble bicycle. After the development of the 'safety' bike in 1885, the bicycle was soon adopted by the working population in large numbers as a convenient and cheap way of travelling to and from work. Among many others, bicycles were made in Bolton by Hugh Cooper of Bradshawgate and Great Moor Street, and by J.E. Jones of Chorley New Road, Horwich.

Swain & Phillipson of Astley Bridge brought out a puncture-proof bicycle tyre in 1892, but it did not take on. Bicycles were also used for light local deliveries. Slightly heavier goods were carried on specially made tricycles, with two youths or men seated side by side. Coopers made a motorised version of a bicycle, called a quadricycle, driven by a 2½hp petrol engine.

Commercial road transport by self-propelled vehicles can be traced back in Bolton to 1899, when Leyland steam lorries appeared on the roads, followed by petrol-driven lorries two years later. Several improvements to these early vehicles were made in following years. In 1919 Maurice Edwards patented a hydraulically operated tipping gear for trucks, and with John H. Bromilow founded Edbro plc, the commercial vehicle body builders. Steam-driven vehicles were eventually superseded by internal combustion engines, although in the 1922 traffic census 219 steam vehicles were recorded, but outnumbered by 3,250 internal combustion vehicles.[9]

Bolton tram repair shed. *(Author's Collection)*

The horse continued to be used for many years, particularly for local deliveries such as coal and milk to households, beer to public houses, and so on. Photographs of busy town centre streets, taken well into the 1930s, often show a sprinkling of horses pulling carts and vans among trams, buses and motor vehicles.

The preserved horse-drawn stagecoach and Bolton electric tram have already been mentioned. Some early motor cars of the types which ran on Bolton roads in the early twentieth century are owned by local car enthusiasts, and can be seen in action on the annual Bolton vintage car rallies usually held in May. Preserved examples of vintage Leyland buses once operated by Bolton Corporation Transport can be seen in the Museum of Transport, Boyle Street, Manchester, and in the Leyland Commercial Vehicle Museum, Leyland.

The Shifnall Street tram depot, which faced onto Bradshawgate, was demolished in 1984, and its site is now occupied by a car showroom, offices and shop. Part of the tramcar repair depot, opened in 1913 in Carlton Street, still exists. After the trams ceased to run, the building became the Corporation motor bus depot until 1979, and is now in multiple occupancy. A plaque on the wall records that the foundation stone was laid in December 1911. The original five tall doorways through which the trams, then double-decker buses, once passed still remain, though they are now largely bricked up. On Chorley New Road, in Horwich, a former tram shed with passenger waiting room alongside survives between Beatrice Street and Mottram Street. Dated 1900, it is now occupied by a tyre dealer. The building that housed the electricity generating plant in Spa Road still stands. A final reminder of the trams is the Tramways Hotel, 307 Blackburn Road. It was built in 1880 on the route operated at first by horse trams and later by electric trams, which form the subject of its inn sign.

Chapter 18

THE MANCHESTER, BOLTON & BURY CANAL & FLETCHER'S CANAL

C oal made the Industrial Revolution, and the need for coal built the canals. So wrote
Charles Hadfield in his book *The Canal Age*, and the situation in south Lancashire
was no different. Manchester needed an increasing quantity of coal for its mill
engines as the end of the eighteenth century approached. When the Bridgwater canal
opened to the city in 1765 the cost of coal halved, and this showed the great advantage
that water transport held over that by road. The coalfield to the north and north-west of
Manchester had not been fully exploited because of the cost of carrying the coal over the
poor roads into the city. Plans were made in 1790 to build a canal connecting Bolton and
Bury to Manchester, to ease the transport of that untapped coal. Two further advantages
were the improved transport of raw cotton to the towns and the dispatch of finished goods
to Manchester.

The route for the canal was surveyed, and successful negotiations with landowners
resulted in an Act of Parliament being passed in May 1791. Work commenced immediately,
with Charles Roberts as canal engineer, replaced by John Nightingale in 1793.[1] Gangs
of navvies dug out the canal in sections, which were eventually joined up. Materials were
moved by wheelbarrows, horses and carts. The canal took six years to complete. In plan, the
canal is Y-shaped, with a 4¾-mile branch to Bury, a 2¾-mile branch to Bolton, and a 6½-
mile stretch to the Manchester terminus, which actually lies in Salford.

The Manchester, Bolton & Bury Canal Navigation started as a narrow canal with
7ft-wide locks. Meanwhile, the Leeds & Liverpool Canal, begun in 1770, was being built
and was seeking a connection with the city of Manchester. Soon after work had commenced
on the M.B & B. Canal, the proprietors proposed that an extension should be built from
the Bolton end to join the L. & L. at a point in the Blackrod/Horwich area. This would
enable L. & L. traffic to reach Manchester via the M.B & B. canal, with the latter gaining
revenue from the tolls charged. The L. & L. Canal was broad, with 14ft-wide locks, so
it was necessary to widen the M.B & B. to take the wide L. & L. boats. The canal was
widened, and the locks already installed were rebuilt, but the proposed extension never
materialised, and the scheme fell through. The L. & L. company later made its connection
to Manchester via the Bridgwater Canal.[2]

By the time the M.B & B. was completed, many new coal pits had been sunk along its length, some with their own short canal branch to the pit loading wharf. Others had short tramroads to the canalside, often gravity operated. As well as coal, canal traffic included lime, salt, pottery and building materials such as timber, bricks and stone. In 1796, although the canal was not quite finished, a passenger packet boat service started from Church Wharf, the Bolton terminus, to Bury and to Manchester. This ran for forty years, up to the opening of the Manchester to Bolton Railway.

Water supply to the canal presented many difficulties. A reservoir was built at Elton, near Radcliffe, to supply the canal. The reservoir drew water via a feeder channel from a point upstream on the River Irwell near Burrs, Bury. Water pumped from adjoining mines was also used.

Once the Manchester to Bolton Railway was running, traffic on the canal rapidly declined. The canal was legally closed to navigation by an Act of Parliament in 1961, though through-traffic had effectively ended after a collapse near the junction of the Bolton and Bury branches in 1936. The canal gradually fell into total disuse. Some stretches were filled in or drained, and the towpath was left to anglers, walkers and wildlife.

The canal company was itself responsible for building the Manchester to Bolton Railway. In 1830 it proposed converting the canal into a railway. This was found to be impractical, and so the railway was built alongside the canal to Clifton, and then on the opposite side of the Croal/Irwell to Bolton. The company now became the Manchester, Bolton & Bury Canal Navigation and Railway Co. The railway opened in 1838, and the canal remained in use. Within ten years the railway had become part of the Lancashire & Yorkshire Railway.

Concentrating on those parts of the canal which lie within the Bolton area, some interesting features can still be seen. The Bolton terminus close to St Peter's Church, after lying derelict for many years, has disappeared under St Peter's Way (A666). The first feature visible travelling towards Manchester is the remains of the three-arch Damside aqueduct at Darcy Lever, which once carried the canal across the River Croal and Radcliffe Road. The aqueduct was demolished in 1965 using gelignite, as it was believed to be in a dangerous condition. The outline of the canal cross-section can still be made out in the remaining side wall of the road arch. The canal is filled in at this point, but a record remains in the name of nearby Aqueduct Street. There were two more aqueducts further along. The first, known as Fogg's aqueduct, spanned a small road leading to Fogg's pit (closed 1913), and the second, Hall Lane or Farnworth aqueduct, carried the canal across the road which leads from Farnworth to Little Lever. Both have disappeared.

Just south of Hall Lane, the next stretch of canal is still watered. About ¾ mile further on is the point where the Bury branch joins at Prestolee. Some canalside buildings remain, which were once the lock-keeper's cottage, canal maintenance workshops and stores, and a flight of locks which led down to the Manchester stretch, 85ft lower. The flight was built as two sets of three staircase locks, with a very short pound between the two sets – six locks altogether. A steep footpath, which once had a wooden roof, runs alongside the locks.[3] In the days of the packet boats, passengers disembarked at the locks and walked along the path to join another boat waiting on the next stretch of the canal. This saved the time needed for a boat to negotiate the locks, and also helped to conserve water. The locks are dry today, and covered with vegetation, but plans have been made to restore them eventually.

Top lock, Prestolee. This is the top lock of the staircase of three locks, which are in need of restoration. *(Author's Collection)*

A realistic account of an imaginary journey on a packet boat from Bolton to Manchester is described in A. Waterson's *On the Manchester, Bolton and Bury Canal*. A scale model of the locks is displayed in Bolton Museum.

The end of the Manchester stretch of the canal below the locks has a basin known as Nob End. It was given this strange name because of the knob-like shape of the basin. The faint outline of a boat-repair dock can be seen close by. The final aqueduct in the Bolton area is the Prestolee aqueduct, where the River Irwell is spanned by a four-arch aqueduct that still contains water. There were further locks at Ringley and at Giant's Seat. Other features spaced along the canal are the milestones, giving the distance from Manchester in quarter miles. The occasional stop grooves can be seen in the stone edges where stop planks could be inserted at strategic points to close off sections of the canal, so that it could be drained for maintenance purposes.

Returning to that part of the Bury branch which lies within our area, some interesting features can be seen from the canal towpath. Like the Bolton branch, there are no locks on the Bury branch, as it follows the same contour level from the top of Prestolee locks all the way to its original terminus. A few hundred feet east of the locks, a serious breach on the south bank of the canal occurred in June 1936, when hundreds of tons of earth and stone from the embankment were washed into the Irwell, some 85ft below. The breach emptied the canal for several miles, and some boats were destroyed, with one left balanced dangerously with one end in the air suspended over the river. The breach was never repaired, since in 1936 very little traffic passed that spot and the expense involved could not be justified. The river was cleared, and a new path made around the breach. The site of the disaster can still be seen. The canal was refilled with water from Bury to just beyond Ladyshore Colliery so that coal could be transported to Bury, until the colliery closed in 1951. This final stretch to Bury remains in water.

Adjacent to the former Mount Sion Bleachworks on the towpath stand the vandalised remains of a late-nineteenth-century steam crane, built by Smith & Sons of Leeds. This was used to unload coal from coal boats directly into the bleachworks. The canal continues to Bury, but is now outside the area. After lying derelict and abandoned for many years, efforts are now being made to restore the canal. The Manchester, Bolton & Bury Canal Society was formed in 1987, with the aim of restoring as much as possible for recreational use, and much progress has already been made, particularly at the Bury end.

The Bolton and Bury branches of the Manchester, Bolton and Bury canal were built close to the Rivers Irwell and Croal. They were cut into the valley sides, in places somewhat

Model of Prestolee canal locks. *(Author's Collection)*

precariously, and high embankments were needed for support. To provide as much ground support as possible the towpath was always on the river side, with the canal furthest from the drop down to the river bed. Considering the period in which it was built, it is a remarkable piece of civil engineering.

The second canal described in this chapter is Fletcher's private canal. Although just outside our area, and only about 1¼ miles long, it connects with the M.B & B. Canal, and is of historical interest. It was constructed by Matthew Fletcher (1731–1808)[4] to convey coal from Wet Earth and Botany Bay Collieries on to the M.B & B. Canal at the Clifton aqueduct.[5] First cut in about 1790 as a crude, narrow canal without stone sides, it runs parallel with the south bank of the River Irwell from a loading bay at Wet Earth, with a branch to Botany Bay Colliery. A year or two later, when the construction of the main canal had reached Clifton, it was extended to a junction close to the aqueduct. A shallow lock on Fletcher's Canal was needed at the joining point, as Fletcher's Canal was cut about 12in higher than the main canal.

Water for Fletcher's Canal was taken from Brindley's feeder to Wet Earth (see Chapter 8), and water from Fletcher's Canal was used to work the Botany Bay winding wheel. Fletcher's Canal was in use for almost 150 years transporting coal, but now lies derelict and half-forgotten. The remains of some of the old coal boats can still be seen lying rotting in the canal.[6] Coal was carried in wooden boxes in the boats for ease of unloading – an early example of containerisation.

Chapter 19

EARLY RAILWAYS

The first railways originated in mines. Miners discovered that it was much easier to push or pull loaded trucks along smooth rails, which also guided them along. Horses were used, as well as human muscle, to move the trucks, and railed tracks outside the mine entrance guided the trucks to unloading points. The concept of the modern railway developed from these early ideas, and steam locomotives were developed to replace animal power. The early colliery railways (or wagonways) were used to move coal from the mine to a wharf, where it could be loaded onto boats or barges, but public railways could carry freight of all kinds, including passengers.

Raw cotton for the mills of Bolton had to be transported from Liverpool, and finished goods for export used the same port. In the late eighteenth and early nineteenth centuries the roads were bad, so waterways were used instead. The Mersey & Irwell Navigation Co. linked Liverpool to Manchester by the two named rivers, and after 1797 the Manchester, Bolton & Bury Canal provided the final link to Bolton. Freight charges were very high, and serious delays often occurred at Liverpool. It was claimed that it often took longer to bring cotton from Liverpool to Bolton than to bring it all the way across the Atlantic by sailing ship!

The pioneering railways in the north-east of England were very successful. Industrialists in Bolton noticed this, and proposed building a railway between Liverpool and the town to speed up transport between the two and reduce the cost. The first step was to make a rail link from Bolton to the Leeds & Liverpool Canal at Leigh, where a branch to the main line of the canal had opened in 1821. This would bypass the Mersey & Irwell Navigation Co.'s river route and the Manchester, Bolton & Bury Canal.

An Act of Parliament was obtained in March 1825, the Bolton & Leigh Railway Company was formed, and George Stephenson (1781–1848) was appointed chief engineer for the line.[1] His brother Robert (b. 1788) also worked on the construction of the line under George's supervision.[2] The line first opened for freight in August 1828 but only from Lecturer's Close, Bolton, as far as Chequerbent, a distance of a few miles. An additional Act was needed in March 1828, to complete the line to Leigh. This was needed as the route had been changed, and the original estimate was too low. The final cost was around £68,000.

The cost of coal in Bolton was soon reduced by 2s a ton.[3] The full route from Bolton to the Liverpool & Leeds Canal at Leigh opened in 1829. Meanwhile, the Liverpool to Manchester Railway was being built, so in August 1829 the Kenyon & Leigh Junction Railway Co. was formed to extend the Bolton to Leigh line to join the Liverpool and Manchester line at Kenyon. This gave a continuous rail link from Bolton to Liverpool, and also a circuitous route from Bolton to Manchester. In 1836 the Kenyon and Leigh junction line was leased to the Bolton & Leigh Co. for twenty-five years.[4]

Stone block sleeper, Bolton & Leigh Railway. *(Author's Collection)*

The Bolton & Leigh Railway had originally been conceived as a goods line, but passenger traffic to Liverpool began in July 1830. On the official opening day (13 June 1831) an estimated 40,000 people watched the arrival in Bolton of the new steam-driven 'iron horse'.[5] The Bolton & Leigh Railway was the first true railway in Lancashire, and predated the more famous Liverpool & Manchester line by two years.

The line from Bolton to Leigh was 7½ miles long, a single track of 4ft 8½in gauge with malleable iron rails set on stone block sleepers. Two inclines were needed in the Bolton area to overcome the contours of the route. The incline at Daubhill was at 1 in 33 to 1 in 38; the other at Chequerbent was at 1 in 49 to 1 in 30. Stationary steam engines pulled the trucks, carriages and the locomotive up the incline, using ropes, as the inclines were too steep for the locomotives of the day to cope with. A 20hp engine operated the Daubhill incline, and a 50hp engine was used at Chequerbent. The locomotive then hauled the train over the relatively level stretches on either side of the inclines. The first terminus of the railway in Bolton was in Great Moor Street. The original station was demolished in 1875 and a new, larger station built on the same site. This 'new' station has also since been demolished.

The first locomotive to run on the Bolton & Leigh Railway was the *Lancashire Witch*, built by Robert Stephenson, George's son (1803–59) at his works in Newcastle upon Tyne. The company bought Timothy Hackworth's *Sans Pareil* from the Liverpool & Manchester Railway soon after the famous Rainhill trials. Next followed the *Union*, built by Rothwell, Hick & Rothwell of Bolton, and the *Salamander* and *Veteran*, by Crook & Dean of Bolton. Hick Hargreaves also later made locomotives for the railway.

The Bolton & Leigh and the Leigh & Kenyon Junction, together with the Liverpool & Manchester Railway, eventually amalgamated with the Grand Junction Railway to become part of the London & North Western Railway. The Daubhill and Chequerbent inclines were abandoned when a new LNWR double-track deviation was opened in February 1885. The line closed in 1954.

Sketch of a 4-2-4 loco built in Bolton in 1854; built by Rothwell & Co. for the 7ft gauge Bristol to Exeter Railway. Eight locos were built, one of which achieved the then record speed of 81.8mph, in 1854. They had the largest driving wheels (9ft diameter) in regular use on British railways. *(Author's Collection)*

Crossing-keeper's house, Bolton & Leigh Railway. The level crossing of 1828, across what is now the A6, was controlled by a keeper who lived in this house. *(Author's Collection)*

Sans Pareil ran on the Bolton to Leigh line for eleven years, and then became the power source for a colliery pump. It was later restored to its original form by John Hick (1815–94), and presented to the Science Museum in South Kensington, London. Bolton Museum also has a model of this locomotive.

Very little of the original route of the Bolton & Leigh Railway is still visible today. Much has been built over, although traces of the trackbed can still be seen in some places. An embankment, known locally as Stephenson's embankment, can be seen close to the M61 motorway, at Junction 5 (A58). Where the original 1829 route crossed the A6 at Chequerbent a house, called Hope House, was once the crossing keeper's cottage.[6]

After the success of the early railways, many new ones were built in the following forty years. Lines from Bolton to nearby towns were opened as listed below. Over a third of the railways in Britain have since been closed, and nearly half the stations, several under Dr Beeching. Many of the disused routes have been converted to other purposes, such as industry and housing, or for footpaths and cycleways.[7]

Line	Opened
Bolton–Salford/Manchester	1838
Bolton–Chorley/Preston	1841
Bolton–Wigan/Liverpool	1848
Bolton–Bury/Heywood	1848, closed 1970
Bolton–Sough/Blackburn	1848
Blackrod–Hindley	1868, closed 1960
Blackrod–Horwich branch	1868, closed 1965
Bolton–Worsley	1875, closed 1954
Astley Bridge Branch	1877, closed 1979
Bradley Fold–Radcliffe	1879, closed 1964

The Manchester, Bolton & Bury Canal Navigation Co. built the Manchester to Bolton line. This is unusual, as later on railway companies bought competing canals, and in some cases closed them down. The line later became part of the Lancashire and Yorkshire Railway. Farnworth station was at first named Tunnel station, taking its name from the nearby 290yd-long tunnel. The tunnel is probably one of the earliest railway tunnels built. The present Trinity Street station was built in 1869/70, replacing an earlier one, though the current platform buildings date from a further rebuilding at the turn of the century. The second station at Great Moor Street was opened in September 1874 by the LNWR to coincide with the new line to Worsley. This was demolished some years after the line closed. A number of smaller stations have been closed.[8]

In several places the railways crossed existing roads by bridges or viaducts. One worthy of mention is that near St Peter's Church. It is constructed of cast iron, with six ribs, each in three sections bolted together to form an arched bridge over what is now St Peter's Way (A666). The bridge was built by Ogle, Sons & Co. of Preston in 1847, for the old Bolton to Blackburn line. Several viaducts in the area are also worthy of mention.

Armsgrove Viaduct, stone-built, 1847, on the Bolton to Blackburn line above an arm of the Wayoh Reservoir.

Folds Road Viaduct, stone-built, 1847. This forks into two: one arm carried the line to the Back o' th' Bank power station and Astley Bridge (track now removed); the other is the Bolton to Blackburn line, which is still in use.

Burnden Viaduct, wrought-iron lattice girder, 1848, which carries the former Bolton to Bury line (closed 1970) across St Peter's Way (A666).

Locomotive sheds were located north of Plodder Lane in Farnworth (opened 1875 and closed 1954), and alongside Crescent Road in Burnden (opened 1879 and closed 1968). A LNWR railway goods warehouse (demolished in 1963) once stood on Deansgate next to the White Lion pub, reached by an extension line from the first Great Moor Street station. The Lancashire & Yorkshire Railway opened another warehouse on Manchester Road, close to Trinity Street main-line station, demolished in 1984. These warehouses handled goods in transit, such as bales of raw cotton coming into Bolton and finished goods awaiting dispatch.

A number of short railways were built to transport coal, stone, clay, and so on. These were known as mineral railways, and were usually owned by private companies

Crankshaw's Winter Hill tramroad, which brought clay down to Crankshaw's pipeworks from a mine on the moor. The track bed can just be seen in the centre. *(Author's Collection)*

and collieries. Some mineral lines were built to the standard gauge of 4ft 8$\frac{1}{2}$in and were connected to the main-line system. Other mineral lines had non-standard gauges and were independent of the public system, and are generally known as tramways or tram roads. Some utilised steam power, but many relied on horse-drawn haulage.

Two examples of early tram roads are worth mentioning. Smithills coal pits were once connected to the Halliwell Bleachworks by a tram road during the first part of the nineteenth century (*c.* 1801–25). The tram road was always horse-drawn and had a limited life, apparently being relocated several times. The rails have been removed, and were cut up into lengths to serve as posts for a fence along part of Smithills Dean Road; they can still be seen today. The track bed can also be traced in a few places, and some of the original stone sleepers have been built into a wall.[9] A tram road brought clay and coal from drifts on Winter Hill (Wildersmoor Mine), down to Crankshaw's Pipe Works at Horwich[10] (called the Klondike Works). This can still be traced, though the site of the works is now a housing estate. An endless chain running between the rails and hooking onto the tubs, powered by a steam engine, operated the system. The gauge of the tram road is unknown, but was probably around 2ft, or slightly less. Many collieries near the Manchester, Bolton & Bury Canal had lines from the pit to the canal where they had their own loading wharves. Other collieries had extensive sidings with connections to the main line, and owned their own coal wagons.[11]

The above paragraphs are only an introduction to the railways in the Bolton area. There are many books for the railway enthusiast which give a more detailed history. A short selection of the books and article dealing specifically with Bolton is listed in Further Reading.

PUBLIC UTILITIES

This chapter deals mainly with water, gas and electricity supplies provided for public use by domestic, commercial and industrial consumers. Reference is also made to the private water supplies of industrial undertakings.

WATER

Water is stored in reservoirs so that a continuous and regulated supply is available at all times, except in periods of prolonged drought. Short-term drought can usually be accommodated by gradually lowering the water level, which is restored to its original depth when the drought ends. Rivers, streams and springs provide the usual sources of water for a reservoir, and river valleys are generally dammed to form man-made lakes. Most reservoirs are built at a level that is higher than the point where the water is used, so the water can flow through the pipelines under gravity. In Bolton, this means that most reservoirs lie to the north and north-west of the town, where the ground is higher. The water can be used for domestic, commercial or industrial purposes, and also to dispose of sewage. Before the nineteenth century, water in Bolton was drawn mostly from wells, and sewage disposal was inadequate, which meant that living conditions were extremely unhealthy. As the population increased, steps were taken to provide reserves of water, and the first reservoirs were constructed.

The Great & Little Bolton Waterworks Co. built the first reservoirs in Bolton – Belmont and Springs Reservoirs. Construction began in 1823 and ended in 1827. Both were fed by the Eagley Brook,[1] and their water at that time was mostly used by industry – bleachers, mills, paper works, and so on. Construction of the Turton & Entwistle Reservoir started in 1830, and was completed by 1840. It was financed by a group of bleachers to regulate the supply of water they drew from the Bradshaw Brook. Its earth dam is 360ft long and 108ft high, and when built was the highest in England. The population of Bolton had grown rapidly by the mid-nineteenth century, and the town desperately needed more water. The Corporation forced the owners of the Turton & Entwistle Reservoir to sell it to them under an Act of 1864. The reservoir provided an instant solution to the Corporation's pressing problem. Water was diverted away from the Bradshaw Brook, and this interfered with the riperian rights of downstream users of the brook.[2] The Corporation built the Wayoh Reservoir as compensation in 1866–76. The capacity of the Wayoh was doubled in 1962.

The Dingle Reservoir was built on Bolton Moor in about 1842, and Rumworth Lodge was constructed in the same period. Robert Heywood (1786–1866) largely instigated the construction of Rumworth Lodge, which was built by the poor and unemployed men of the town. Free water was supplied to the poorest part of the town through standpipes in the streets.[3]

In 1847 Liverpool Corporation obtained an Act to construct the Rivington and Anglezarke Reservoirs to store water for the city. The engineer in charge was Thomas Hawksley (1807–93), and by 1857 the first water was supplied by gravity to Prescot in a cast-iron underground pipe 44in in diameter. Many of the navvies who constructed the reservoirs were Irish. They lived in makeshift camps around the area, and it is reported that they terrorised the local population with their drunken behaviour. Hawksley designed and built a sand-filter water-treatment plant at the lower end of Lower Rivington Reservoir, which when built was the largest in the world.[4] A modern water-treatment plant has recently replaced it, at a cost of some £39 million. The dams of these reservoirs are built of earth with a puddled clay core. They are known as gravity dams, since they rely on their dead weight to resist the pressure of water. The sides facing the water are lined with stone to protect them from erosion. In 1875 the Yarrow Reservoir was built and connected to Anglezarke Reservoir to increase the storage capacity. Two other reservoirs at Roddlesworth (actually just outside the Bolton area) are also connected to the Rivington system via an open channel, called the Goit.

Two more reservoirs built in the early and mid-twentieth century are the Delph (1911–21) and the Jumbles (1967–70). The latter is a compensation reservoir for the Bradshaw Brook, and this allowed the Turton & Entwistle and Wayoh Reservoirs to supply drinking water. Delph Reservoir supplies compensation and drinking water. Some of the reservoirs mentioned are also used for leisure pursuits, such as sailing and fishing. Bolton also takes water from the Thirlmere to Manchester pipeline, which crosses the area underground on its way to Manchester. Nothing of the pipe can be seen on the surface; it lies between the locomotive works and the south side of Chorley New Road, in Horwich.

As well as the reservoirs described above, there are some small named reservoirs that were built by industrialists for their own exclusive use. Doffcocker Lodge is an example. It was built to provide water for Mortfield Bleachworks (demolished) about a mile away, via the Doffcocker Brook. At the works were more reservoirs storing water. Victoria Lake, which supplied water to Halliwell Bleachworks, is another example, and the Ornamental Reservoir at Belmont supplies water to Springside Paper Mill.

There were scores of unnamed small reservoirs or lodges adjacent to mills. They were used to supply cooling water for the engine condenser. Water was drawn from the Corporation mains to make up for any lost by evaporation. Most of these have been filled in, and they often now form the mill car park. A few remain in water, and are often used for fishing.

Another important use of water since the mid-to late Victorian period is for conveying sewage through underground pipes. Sewage treatment works were then built away from towns and close to a river, where the treated sewage could be discharged.

Before a proper sewerage system was built in Bolton, privy middens, dry-earth closets, bucket closets and cesspits were used to dispose of human waste. The closet containers were emptied every week or so by night soil men, and the contents carted away for dumping in the Croal or some other watercourse, or for use as fertiliser. The overcrowding, squalor and insanitary conditions let to epidemics of typhoid and cholera, causing many deaths.

The Council authorities and medical officers gradually realised that public health would be greatly improved by better methods for disposing of human waste and liquid

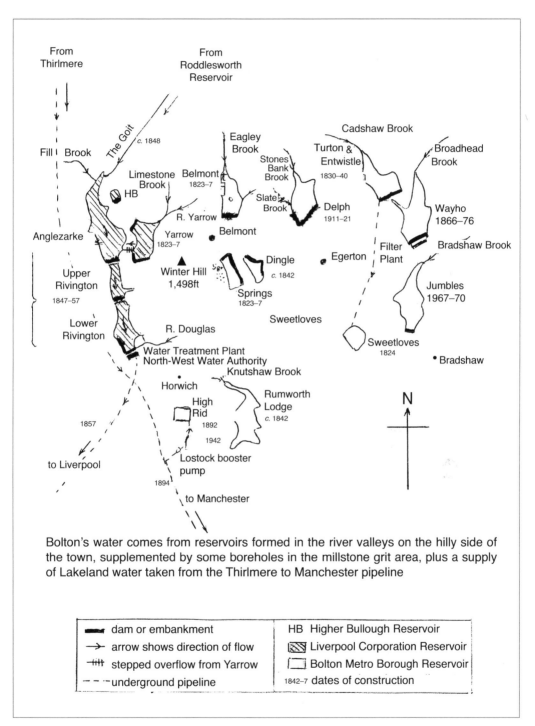

Bolton's water comes from reservoirs formed in the river valleys on the hilly side of the town, supplemented by some boreholes in the millstone grit area, plus a supply of Lakeland water taken from the Thirlmere to Manchester pipeline

A sketch of the main reservoirs in the area. *(Author's Collection)*

Doffcocker Nature Reserve, originally a reservoir for Cross's Bleachworks, incorporating Doffcocker Brook in the 1850s. The nature reserve is managed by Bolton Metropolitan Borough Council. It is a good example of an old industrial site that has been turned into a place for public leisure and enjoyment. *(Author's Collection)*

factory waste. Instead of leaving this to lie for long periods, it should be removed as soon as possible. Water flowing through sewer pipes with branches to houses, factories, street drains and so on carried the waste away.

In the 1890s it was recommended that new houses should have indoor water closets connected to the sewerage system, and that older houses should also be connected. An outfall sewage works had already been built in Hacken Lane, Darcy Lever, between 1884 and 1886, from which the treated effluent was discharged into the Croal. The sewage was treated in settling tanks by filtration and chemical methods. Today the site is a car park for the Croal/Irwell Valley Country Park. Another sewage works, built in 1881, off Hall Lane, Farnworth, also discharged into the Croal. This site is partly covered today by a caravan park. A large sewage works just inside Bolton's boundary is on Red Rock Lane, Kearsley, and discharges into the Irwell. Small sewage works were once scattered around Bolton, such as those at Bradshaw and Eagley, which only dealt with their immediate area.

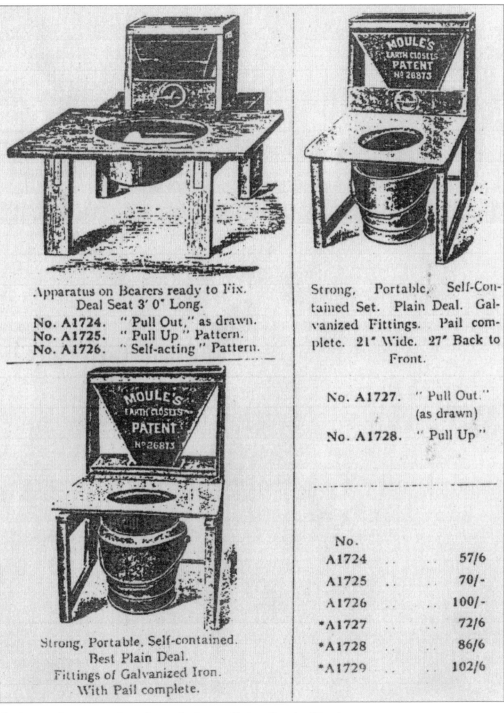

Apparatus on Bearers ready to Fix.
Deal Seat 3' 0" Long.

No. A1724. " Pull Out," as drawn.
No. A1725. " Pull Up " Pattern.
No. A1726. " Self-acting " Pattern.

Strong, Portable, Self-Contained Set. Plain Deal. Galvanized Fittings. Pail complete. 21" Wide. 27" Back to Front.

No. A1727. " Pull Out."
(as drawn)

No. A1728. " Pull Up "

Strong, Portable, Self-contained.
Best Plain Deal.
Fittings of Galvanized Iron.
With Pail complete.

No.		
A1724	.. ..	57/6
A1725	.. ..	70/-
A1726	.. ..	100/-
*A1727	.. ..	72/6
*A1728	.. ..	86/6
*A1729	.. ..	102/6

A nineteenth-century advert for earth closets. *(Bolton Evening News)*

A reconstructed Victorian brick sewer large enough to walk through is in the 'Underground Manchester' feature at the Museum of Science & Industry. It contains examples of early lavatories, such as tipplers, and other sanitary ware similar to that once used in Bolton.

GAS

Coal gas, commonly called town gas, is made by the destructive distillation of low-ash coal in externally fired retorts. After being drawn off from the retort, the crude gas is purified and cooled before being stored in large cylindrical gas holders. The residue from the retorts is coke, which is itself a useful fuel for other purposes. Other valuable by-products, such as tar, are extracted during the cooling and purification processes. Initially gas manufacturers preferred to use cannel coal, until this became too scarce and expensive. Much of the cannel coal used in Bolton gasworks came from the Wigan coalfield.

William Murdoch (1754–1839) was engaged in erecting steam engines for Boulton & Watt in Cornwall. In 1792 he first carried out experiments on using coal gas for lighting and succeeded in lighting his house. The light came from open-flame jets. Murdoch's pioneering ideas were developed, and gas-making plants began to appear all over the country. By about 1860 there were some 900 independent gas-making companies in Britain. Initially, gas was used for lighting, but its heating properties were not utilised in those early days.

Many cotton mills in Bolton adopted gas lighting, and built their own small gas-works.[5] Gas lighting was safer than the candles and oil lamps used previously, which had presented a greater fire risk. Some mills piped gas from their gas plant to the cottages they had built for their own workforce.[6] An example of this was Dean Mills at Barrow Bridge. Gas was also used in some mills for the singeing process. This involved rapidly passing cloth or thread across a bank of burning gas jets. Any raised small fibres or hairs were burnt off, and the appearance of the finished product was improved.

Gas was soon used to light streets, houses and public places. The gas was supplied from a central gas works through underground piping. On Barrow Bridge Road, some old cast-iron lamp-posts survive. These were once lit by gas, but have now been converted to electricity. The Bolton Gas Lighting Co. was established in 1818.[7] By May 1819 there were eighteen gas lamps on Bradshawgate and Deansgate. The offices of the Bolton Gas Co. were in Hotel Street, about 500yds from the gas works. In 1878 they housed Bolton's first telephone.[8] In Farnworth a pioneer provider of town gas was James Berry, who made gas in a small way on Market Street for local distribution. The Farnworth & Kearsley Gas Co. first produced gas from their Crowbank works in 1855. All the Bolton gas works were taken over by Bolton Corporation in 1872. Britain's gas industry was nationalised in 1949. Gas making declined rapidly after about 1965, as town gas was replaced by North Sea gas.

By the last quarter of the nineteenth century electricity began to replace gas lighting, but gas continued to be used for heating, by both industrial and domestic consumers. The domestic gas cooker began to appear in about 1870. The incandescent gas mantle was invented in 1885, and was soon adopted, as it gave more light and greatly reduced the risk of fires.

A decorative gas lamp-standard and a horse trough by Rothwell, Hick & Rothwell in Old Market Place, late nineteenth century. It was eventually removed because of increased traffic in the area. Old Market Place is now called Town Hall Square. *(Bolton Evening News)*

The main features of the gas manufacturing industry that survive today are the large gas holders, where gas is stored under a constant pressure. These were designed to accommodate changing volumes of gas by using sliding sections, which telescoped one into the other. They were made from wrought-iron or mild-steel plates, riveted together to form large-diameter open-ended drums. They usually had three sections, the top one with a domed roof. The bottom section had the largest diameter and the top section the smallest. The top and middle sections telescoped into the bottom section to give the smallest volume. As more gas was made the top and middle sections rose to accommodate the increased volume. Water seals surrounded the sliding joints and prevented any escape of gas. There are two basic designs. The oldest dates from an 1824 patent, in which the sections rose and fell vertically inside a number of outer supporting columns, which carried guide-rails. The moving sections had grooved wheels attached to their outer circumference, which ran along these rails. The gas holders at the Spa Road gas works are of this design. The other design, introduced in about 1890, is the spiral lift holder in which spiral guides are fitted around the circumference of each section. As each section rises or falls, it twists as it follows the guides. Vertical columns are not needed in this design. Gas holders even out fluctuations in gas

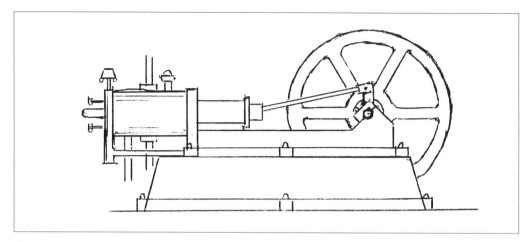

A sketch of a horizontal gas engine, *c.* 1890. Town gas was first used for lighting, but by about 1875 gas engines began competing against steam engines. Their popularity was shortlived, however, as electric power soon replaced them. *(Author's Collection)*

Gas holders, Spa Road. *(Author's Collection)*

demand, allowing the gas-making plant to run at a constant load. The gas works are now closed and the gas holders redundant. The buildings that housed the retorts, purification plants and so on have been demolished, and the gas holders will also go, where they have not been granted the status of a listed building. The railway sidings adjacent to the gas works, which once brought in coal and took out coke, have also been removed.

Coal gas was also used for balloon ascents in the early part of the nineteenth century. In 1826 Charles Green made an ascent from a point next to the Moor Lane gas works, using coal gas as the lifting medium. Other balloon ascents were made for public entertainment at the completion of Blinkhorn's 367ft chimney in 1842, and at the dedication of Samuel Crompton's statue in Nelson Square.

ELECTRICITY

Britain's electricity heritage does not go as far back in history as other local public utilities, cotton spinning or engineering but its development was rapid, and brought about many changes in a comparatively short time. It commenced in 1893, when the foundation stone for the Corporation-owned works was laid in Spa Road next to the existing gas works. Electricity would be generated to supply current for street lighting by the recently invented incandescent carbon filament lamp, which was challenging gas for this purpose.

Within a few years the electricity works was extended to house more generating plant, to provide a 550V direct current for the new tramway system. It had been decided by then that DC was more suitable for traction use. All the generating equipment was driven by steam engines, mostly of inverted vertical design, made locally by firms such as Musgraves, J. & E. Woods and Hick Hargreaves. The dynamos and alternators used were manufactured by Mather & Platt, Ferranti and others. At first, single-phase AC at 83.33 cycles per second was supplied, generated at 2,000V, and transformed in substations to a lower voltage for distribution to users. Three-phase current started in 1906, generated at 6,000V and a frequency of 50 cycles, anticipating what was later adopted as the standard frequency for the whole country.

A peculiarity existed for a while because the Kay Street area and Dobson & Barlow's factory needed the old DC supply, so a building housing rotary converters was built in Duncan Street to make the necessary rectification. This closed in 1939, when the district changed to AC. Duncan Street disappeared when the Gates Retail Park was built.

When Spa Road could no longer cope with the ever-rising demand for electricity, the Corporation built a new 12.5MW station at Back o' th' Bank, which started up in 1914. A three-phase supply at 50 cycles was generated at 6,600V by a Zoelly-type steam turbine. By this date turbines had superceded engines as the preferred prime mover for electrical work.[9]

The 1926 Electricity Supply Act created the national grid system, standardised at 132kVa and 50 cycles, and Back o' th' Bank station was selected as one of the more efficient stations to supply it. The station was extended to provide more power in 1939, and again in 1948. Eventually it closed in 1978, and the site was cleared. However, one turbo-alternator was saved, and is on display in the Power Hall of the Museum of Science & Industry in Manchester.[10] The old Spa Road station still stands, but no longer generates electricity.

Farnworth UDC built an electricity station in Albert Road in 1901, to generate a DC supply for their trams. When the station became overloaded, self-generation was abandoned

Above: Offices fronting the electricity generating station in Spa Road. *(Author's Collection)*

Below: The weathered date of the foundation stone is 13 December 1893. *(Author's Collection)*

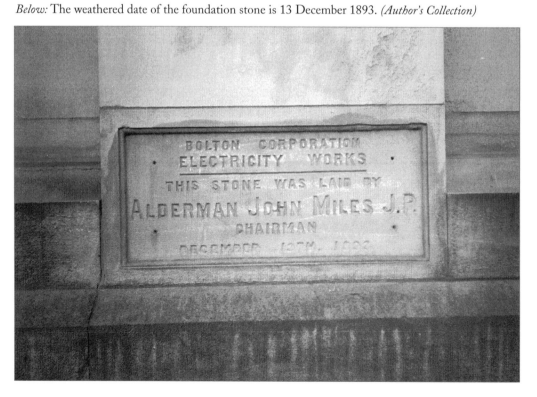

Back o' th' Bank Power Hall. This 30MW steam turbine set ran from 1923 to 1979. When the site was redeveloped in 1981 the set went to the Power Hall of the Manchester Museum of Science & Industry. *(Bolton Evening News)*

and AC was bought in from the Lancashire Electric Power Co., part of which was converted to DC. The station building still stands, but is now part of the NW Electricity Board.

The Lancashire Electric Power Co., which had been supplying electricity in the county since 1905, built a 272MW coal-fired station at Kearsley, officially opening in 1929. It was extended in 1936 and again in 1949, eventually closing in 1985. The site was cleared, and is now partly covered by housing and small industrial units. Some of the old LEP sub-stations may still be found in various parts of Bolton and district. The 1947 Electricity Act nationalised supply in Britain, creating the British Electricity Authority, renamed the Central Electricity Authority, which took control of Back o' th' Bank and Kearsley stations on 1 April 1948.

As electric power became available Bolton mills gradually converted to it, scrapping their steam engines, boilers and so on. At first large electric motors were installed on each floor, driving the existing lineshafts. Later on each machine was fitted with its own electric motor, dispensing entirely with lineshafting and belts. Some of the later-built mills generated their own electricity with small steam turbines, Falcon and Kearsley Mills being examples. Bolton's newest mill, at Astley Bridge, opened in 1926, and took all its power from the

A Musgrave steam engine driving a Ferranti alternator at Southport electricity works. This cross-compound engine from about 1895 is on the right of the alternator, but only one cylinder is visible. The other is hidden by the alternator. *(Northern Mill Engine Society)*

public supply from the outset and was known as 'the electric mill'. Electricity also brought about great changes in people's lives – domestically, commercially and industrially. Many electrical appliances were invented to improve home life, and examples dating from 1900 may be seen in the Electric Gallery of the Museum of Science & Industry. As leisure time increased, owing to shorter working hours, mass entertainment in the cinema resulted. The first purpose-built cinema in Bolton was the Electric Theatre, in Deansgate, opened in 1910. At one time as many as twenty-eight cinemas were operating in Bolton and district. Most have now gone, but the mock Tudor front of the old 'Royal' in St George's Road may still be seen.

The reader will be able to think of many other examples of our electrical heritage – things which have only become possible today through the convenience and cleanliness of electricity. All industries have been affected. Steam power in the manufacturing industry and on the railways is now a thing of the past, although ironically steam is still used for the bulk generation of electricity itself, though other fuels, such as North Sea gas, are replacing coal. Electric power has taken over, and steam engines and locomotives are banished to museums or private preservation societies. The communications and information technology industries depend entirely on electricity. New uses of electricity, or a revival of a former use, such as the electric car, are being investigated today. Electricity has an assured future, providing it can always be generated economically.

Chapter 21

VICTORIAN & EDWARDIAN
BENEVOLENCE

Anumber of master spinners, coal owners and other industrialists used their wealth to present the people of Bolton with benefits and amenities that they still enjoy today. Once his business had built up to a satisfactory profit level and was being run by a competent manager, an industrialist often turned his energies to other matters. He would own a residence appropriate to his social standing, usually located quite close to his factory – in some cases actually within sight of it. He may then decide to enter into public life, and to serve the community by using his time and intellect as a Member of Parliament. Or he may prefer to operate at a local level, by entering the town council and becoming an alderman or mayor. An example of the former is John Hick (1815–94) of the engineering firm Hick Hargreaves, who was MP for Bolton in 1868. An example of the latter is Thomas Ridgway Bridson (1795–1863) of Bolton Bleachworks, who was mayor in 1847.[1]

An industrialist's desire to benefit the community in which he lived could be expressed in other ways. He could, for example, endow a church, give land to the town for a specific purpose, meet the cost of a public building, and so on, as a kind of wealth-sharing exercise. The following paragraphs list some of the philanthropic acts of textile mill owners and others during the Victorian and Edwardian periods. It excludes the paternalism exhibited by some mill owners towards their own workers who provided them with houses, schools and libraries. This was often done to attract a workforce, and was not a benefit enjoyed by the public as a whole. The list is not exhaustive, being restricted to more important gifts and bequests.

Joseph Ridgway (1765–1842), of Wallsuches Bleachworks, contributed to the cost of Holy Trinity Church in Horwich, and helped finance the building of the nearby church school. He also founded a clothing charity for the poor of Horwich. He built Ridgmont House, Chorley Old Road, in about 1801, as his family seat, within sight of the bleachworks. The house has survived, and is now a Masonic Lodge.

William Hesketh Lever (1851–1923), who became Lord Leverhulme in 1917, was probably Bolton's most important benefactor. From humble beginnings in Bolton he built up the well-known firm of Lever Brothers, famous for its Sunlight soap, but his factories were not in Bolton. In 1902 he donated over 2,000 acres of land at Rivington to Bolton Corporation, which now forms the Lever Country Park. He also endowed Bolton School, restored the ruinous Hall i' th' Wood and in 1919 gave Leverhulme Park to the town, the year in which he was mayor of Bolton. His part-time residence was Roynton Cottage, on the slopes of Rivington Pike. The first cottage was burnt down by a suffragette in 1913, and was replaced by a second on the same site. After his death it remained empty, and was finally demolished in 1947. Traces of its floor and foundations can still be seen.

Lord Leverhulme presenting his gift of Heaton playing fields to the people of Bolton in 1922. *(Bolton Evening News)*

The Ainsworth family, who for five generations were the owners of Halliwell Bleachworks and of local coal and fireclay mines, gave many gifts to the town. Among these were the rebuilding of St Peter's Church, Halliwell, meeting the cost of building Jubilee School, Church Road, building St Paul's Place, St Paul's Church, and the associated Church School on Halliwell Road, and converting an old textile workshop into Markland Hill School. Peter Ainsworth (1737–1807), nicknamed 'The Opulent Bleacher' on account of his wealth, bought Smithills Hall and Estate in 1801; the Hall became the family seat. The family also owned Lightbounds House. Both buildings still exist – the Hall is a museum, the house a private residence. Peter Ainsworth (1790–1870) was MP for Bolton.

John Pennington Thomasson, owner of Mill Hill Mills, bequeathed Thomasson or Mere Park, Halliwell, to the people of Bolton in 1889. The park contains Mere Hall, built in about 1836. Thomasson was MP for Bolton in 1853. After his death the Hall saw several uses before closing in 1960. It has been restored, and now houses the Registrar's Office, together with rooms available for public functions.

The Barlow family, of the firm Barlow & Jones, spinners and weavers of Albert, Cobden, Egyptian and Prospect Mills, gave many gifts to the town. Among these were land and a sum of money for the National Children's Home for Destitute Children at Edgworth, donated by James Barlow in 1871. In 1909 the children of James and his wife Alice presented the Barlow Institute, Bolton Road, Edgworth, a bowling green and open-air swimming pool (now gone) for the use of local residents and the general public, in memory of their parents. Barlow Park, Sharples, was also given to the town by the firm. The family residence was Greenthorne on Broadhead Road, built in 1860. James Barlow was mayor of Bolton in 1867/8.

Mere Hall, Halliwell, formerly the home of J.P. Thomasson, owner of Mill Hill Mills. He presented the Hall to the people of Bolton in 1889. It now houses the Registrar's Office. *(S.M. Jones)*

Bolton parish church (another St Peter's) was rebuilt in 1867, the cost being met by **Peter Ormrod** (d. 1875) of the firm Ormrod & Hardcastle, Spinners, of Flash Street mills and Bullfield mill. He was also a banker, and had the nickname 'Ready Money Peter'.[2] The church was built on the site of an earlier medieval church, which had become unsafe to use. Peter's brother James, a co-founder of Ormrod & Hardcastle, lived in Halliwell Lodge, which became a hotel and pub in 1899. The building has now been demolished and replaced by modern housing. James built the original St Luke's Church, on Chorley Old Road; the present building is a replacement, as the original was burnt down in the 1970s.

Stephen Blair (1804–70) of the firm Blair & Sumner, bleachers and finishers at Mill Hill bleachworks, Kestor Street, left money for the erection of Blair Hospital on Hospital Road, Bromley Cross. This is now the Institute of Islamic Higher Education. Stephen Blair was Mayor of Bolton in 1845, and also MP for the Borough. He lived in Mill Hill House.

In 1850 **Edward Carr Deakin** took over part of Ashworth's dye works at Egerton Mill; this ran until closure in 1963. The dye works was demolished, and the site is now the Deakins Industrial Estate, used by a number of small businesses. The Deakin family gave Egerton Park, Blackburn Road, to local people, and a swimming baths and gymnasium in nearby Water Street at about the same time (both have now gone). The Deakins' family residence was Egerton House, now a hotel.

Edmund Potter (d. 1933) of Hall Chemical Works, Little Lever, bequeathed his house, Fernclough, on Chorley New Road, initially as a convalescent home or hospital. It later became a training centre for the town's ambulance service.

Farnworth Park (originally known as the People's Park) was given to the general public in 1864 by **Thomas Barnes** (b. 1813), the owner of Dixon Green Mill. He was also MP for Bolton.

The Lancashire & Yorkshire Railway Co. at Chorley New Road, Horwich, gave money towards the Mechanics' Institute, which was built opposite their works in 1887. It became a technical school, open to the general public, in 1925, but burned down in 1977.

The Earl of Bradford, Bolton landowner, and owner of Great Lever, Raikes and Hacken Collieries, gave land for the erection of Bridgeman Street (now Lower Bridgeman Street) Public Baths, opened in 1846. The building still survives, and is now Bolton Business Centre.

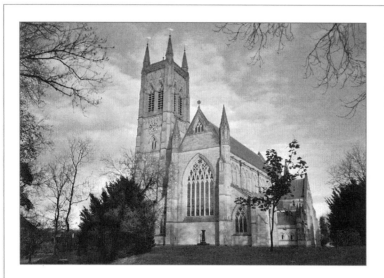

Bolton parish church. Peter Ormrod, a Bolton banker and mill owner, financed the cost of building this church in 1867. *(S.M. Jones)*

Robert Heywood (1786–1868), the son in the firm John Heywood & Son, quilting manufacturers, gave part of the land of the Heywood Recreation Ground, Bridgeman Street, in 1866. Heywood was mayor of Bolton in 1839. **Charles James Darbishire** (1797–1874), business partner of Robert Heywood, gave the recreation ground named after him in 1869. Darbishire was Bolton's first mayor in 1838.

Elizabeth Lum, widow of John Lum (1768–1836), spinner of Mount Pleasant mill, built some almshouses for poor widows with money from her husband's will. The buildings were demolished when Lum Street gas works was extended, but Bolton Corporation replaced them in 1886 by building six new almshouses a mile or so away, at 50–60 Mackenzie Street, Astley Bridge. The houses still exist today, and are known as Mrs Lum's Almshouses.

Bolton Hospital received a number of gifts from industrialists during its history. These commenced in 1827 when land for building a dispensary in Nelson Square was given by the **Earl of Bradford**.[3] That building was the forerunner of the Royal Infirmary on Chorley New Road, opened in 1883. **John Musgrave** (1784–1864) of Musgrave & Sons, Globe Ironworks, Kay Street and Atlas Mills, Chorley Old Road, engineers and spinners, left money towards building the new infirmary. The hospital authorities named a ward after him in appreciation.[4] The site of the old dispensary is now occupied by a shop selling electrical equipment, and the infirmary site is now a sports and leisure centre.

As is shown by the above benefactors, gifts to the town can be divided into four categories – spiritual, recreational, educational, and public health and well-being. Textile mill owners made the greatest contribution, as in Victorian times textiles were Bolton's main industry. Next in number were contributions from the engineering sector, but gifts from coal-mine owners appear meagre by comparison. Perhaps coal mining in Bolton was an industry that did not produce the same wealth or profits as cotton spinning, and many local mines were small enterprises, poorly capitalised. Further research may adjust the balance.

NOTES

CHAPTER 1

1. I. Taylor, *Words and Places: Illustrations of History, Ethnology and Geography*, Dent, 1911, p. 149.
2. W.D. Billington, *From Affetside to Yarrow: Bolton Place Names and their History*, Ross Anderson, 1982, pp. 23–4.
3. A bloomery consisted of a rough bowl-shaped stone-melting hearth with a removable dome made of clay. Small pieces of iron ore were smelted in it, using charcoal as fuel, and the dome was broken open to extract the lump of wrought iron (the bloom). A bloomery was sited where there were plenty of trees for making charcoal, and the iron ore was brought to it. When the surrounding fuel source was used up, the bloomery was abandoned and a fresh one started elsewhere. Remains of the hearth, some clinker, and pieces of iron slag usually mark the spot where a bloomery once existed.

CHAPTER 2

1. A spindle whorl is a circular disk of stone which, when fastened to the free end of a vertically held wooden spindle, acts like a flywheel to prolong the spin of the spindle.
2. A palstave is a kind of axe or chisel which fits into a wooden shaft.
3. C. Aspin, *Transactions of the Lancashire & Cheshire Antiquarian Society*, Vol. 65, 1955, p. 132.
4. D. Mills, *The Placenames of Lancashire*, Batsford, 1976; W.D. Billington, *From Affetside to Yarrow*, Ross Anderson, 1982.
5. J. Gimpel, *The Mediaeval Machine*, Pimlico, 1992, pp. 11–12.
6. Excavations by Manchester University's Archaeological Unit in 1998 discovered evidence of thirteenth-century life in Churchgate, at the site of the former Boar's Head pub.
7. D.R. Mills, *A Short History of Hall i' th' Wood*, published by the author, 1992, p. 21 (mill and kiln of 1635).
8. J.J. Francis, *Lords of the Manor of Bradshaw*, Turton Local History Society, 1977, p. 10 (mill of 1542).
9. A 1620 map of the Smithills Estate shows a 'milne hulme' on the Dean Brook. *A Study of Smithills Estate*, Bolton MBC, no date.
10. J.H. Longworth, *The Cotton Mills of Bolton, 1780–1985*, Bolton Museum, 1987, p. 106 (fulling mill of 1483).
11. J.J. Francis, *Affetside, a Historical Survey*, Turton Local History Society, 1996, p. 3 (fulling mill of 1542).

12. Mills, *A Short History*, p. 9. A 'Walke mylne' of 1550.

13. N.J. Frangopulo, *Tradition in Action*, EP Publishing, 1977, p. 141.

14. *The Textile Industry of Bolton*, Bolton MBC, 1985, p. 7. An alnager was a Crown Inspector of woollen cloth.

15. B. Jones, Note in the *Friends of Smithills Hall Newsletter*, Vol. 1 No. 2, 1996, p. 3.

16. S. Smiles, *The Huguenots*, Murray, 1884, p. 109.

17. A.P. Wadsworth and J. De Lacy Mann, *The Cotton Trade and Industrial Lancashire 1600–1780*, Manchester University Press, 1931, p. 15.

18. Gilbert J. French, *Life and Times of Samuel Crompton*, Kelley, 1970, pp. 4ff.

CHAPTER 3

1. Quoted by Helen Hayes in *Eagley Brook*, Turton Local History Society, 1997, p. 47.

2. *Bolton Chronicle*, 17 May 1979.

3. H. Catling, *The Spinning Mule*, The Lancashire Library, 1986, p. 193.

4. The size of a cotton yarn or thread is denoted by a number called a count, which is the number of hanks of 840 yards that weigh one pound. Counts of between 25 and 50 are termed medium, and counts above 50 are classed as fine, also known as Bolton counts.

5. J.H. Longworth, *The Cotton Mills of Bolton, 1780–1985*, Bolton Museum, 1987, p. 18.

CHAPTER 4

1. A.P. Wadsworth and J. De Lacy Mann, *The Cotton Trade and Industrial Lancashire, 1600–1780*, Manchester University Press, 1931, pp. 261–5.

2. H.C. Collins, *The Roof over Lancashire*, Dent, 1950, p. 5.

3. O. Ashmore, *The Industrial Archaeology of Lancashire*, David & Charles, 1969, p. 27.

4. C.H. Wood, *The History of Wages in the Cotton Trade during the Past Hundred Years*, Manchester University Press, 1910, pp. 127–8.

CHAPTER 5

1. W.D. Billington, *Doffcocker*, Halliwell Local History Society, 1991, p. 10.

2. Anon., *Samuel Crompton and a Short History of Dobson & Barlow*, 1927, pp. 82–3.

3. An illustration of the model appeared in the *Bolton Evening News* on 24 August 1974. The model is presently in Bolton Museum.

4. H. Hayes, *Eagley Brook*, Turton Local History Society, 1997. Langshaw's and Wakefield's, p. 36; New Eagley, p. 47; Longworth, pp. 18–19; Delph, p. 21.

5. D. O'Connor, *Barrow Bridge, Bolton*, Bolton Industrial History Society, 1972, p. 2.

6. W.D. Billington, *Barrow Bridge*, Halliwell Local History Society, 1988, p. 9.

7. J.H. Longworth, *The Cotton Mills of Bolton 1780–1985*, Bolton Museum, 1987. Damside, p. 17; St Helena, pp. 14–15; North Bridge, p. 15.

8. *Turton through the Ages*, Turton Local History Society, p. 20. The mill changed its name to Vale Mill in 1877, and was run by the Edgworth Spinning Co. It closed in 1952.

9. *Ibid.*: Delph Hill, p. 18; Peel, p. 27; Bradshawgate, p. 17; King Street, p. 15.

10. M. Williams and D.A. Farnie, *Cotton Mills in Greater Manchester*, Carnegie, 1992, p. 147.

11. R. Marsden, *Cotton Weaving*, Bell, 1895, pp. 382–4.

12. Longworth, *The Cotton Mills of Bolton*, pp. 79, 80.

13. The sixth annual Mills Conference (*Bolton Evening News*, 8 May 1997).

14. Anon., *150 Facts about Bolton*, leaflet published by Bolton Metropolitan Borough, 1988, Facts 21 and 45.

15. R.N. Holden, *Mill Architects*, Manchester & Region Industrial Archaeological Society Newsletter, No. 83, p. 6.

16. Anon., 'George Temperley & Son', *Little Piecer*, *Journal of the Halliwell Local History Society*, No. 21, 1989.

17. Longworth, *The Cotton Mills of Bolton*, p. 59.

18. M.D. Smith, *About Horwich*, Wyre, p. 33.

19. D. O'Connor, *The Eagley Story*, Richardson, 2000, pp. 11–12.

CHAPTER 6

1. J.H. Longworth, *The Cotton Mills of Bolton, 1780–1985*, Bolton Museum, 1987, p. 79.

CHAPTER 7

1. In 1784 Richard Bateson was transported for seven years; in 1793 Daniel Davies was transported for seven years. James Holland was executed by public hanging on Bolton Moor in 1786 for stealing 30yds of cloth from Thomas Tweat's Burnden bleach croft.

2. The painting is reproduced in black and white in J.H. Longworth's *The Cotton Mills of Bolton*, p. 10.

3. C. Southern, 'The Changing Face of Bolton', *Bolton Evening News*, 12 September 1983.

CHAPTER 8

1. J.J. Francis, *Lords of the Manor of Bradshaw*, Turton Local History Society, 1977, p. 10.

2. J. Boardman, *Records and Traditions of Deane Village, Church and Parish*, 1904.

3. H. Jones, 'Smithills Mill', *Little Piecer*, *Journal of Halliwell Local History Society*, No. 64, 1996. The mill building possibly became part of Halliwell Bleachworks early in the nineteenth century.

4. D.R. Mills, *A Short History of Hall i' th' Wood*, published by the author, 1992, p. 21.

5. R. Lindop, *The History of Turton Mill*, Turton Local History Society, Publication no. 11, 1989, p. 7.

6. J.H. Longworth, *The Cotton Mills of Bolton 1780–1985*, Bolton Museum, 1987, p. 106.

7. J.J. Francis, *Affetside: An Historical Survey*, Turton Local History Society, 1996, p. 3.

8. *Turton Through the Ages*, Turton Local History Society, p. 101.

9. Anon., *A Guide to Lead Mine Clough*, published jointly by GMC, LCC and NWWA, 1984.

10. One of which is in C. Aspin, *Lancashire, the First Industrial Society*, Helmshore Local History Society, 1969, illustration 3.

11. Longworth, *The Cotton Mills of Bolton*, p. 22.

12. A. Morton, *Heaton*, Bolton Environmental Education Project, 1991, p. 1.

13. The name Gal is a shortening of Galloway, a breed of horse used to work a gin for winding and raising coal in a kibble. The gin was superseded by Brindley's scheme.

CHAPTER 9

1. B.T. Barton, 'Historical Gleanings of Bolton and District', *Bolton Chronicle*, first series, 1881, pp. 177–8.
2. J. Clegg, 'Chronological History of Bolton', *Bolton Chronicle*, 1888, p. 65.
3. E. Baines, *History, Directory and Gazetteer of the County Palatine of Lancaster*, Wales & Co., Vol. 2, 1825. Reprinted by David & Charles.
4. An inverted vertical steam engine is called inverted because its cylinders are placed above the crankshaft. Until this design was developed in about 1850, vertical engines had their cylinders on a baseplate with an overhead crankshaft.
5. The Northern Mill Engine Society's collection of stationary steam engines is in a warehouse of the former Atlas Mills, Chorley Old Road. The building is located just beyond the petrol station, on the site now occupied mainly by Morrison's supermarket.
6. A shingling hammer is used to hammer a bloom (or lump) of hot iron just taken out of the furnace and still plastic. It forces out any slag in the bloom, and consolidates the iron into a block.

CHAPTER 10

1. R.H. Parsons, *History of the Institution of Mechanical Engineers*, published by the Institution, 1947, p. 291.
2. G.J. French, *Life and Times of Samuel Crompton*, Kelley, 1970, reprint of 1869 edition, p. 15.
3. One of the first ships to bring frozen meat from New Zealand in 1880 was fitted with Hick Hargreaves air refrigeration equipment.
4. Most information from S. Ferguson, 'Our Triumph of Survival', *Bolton Evening News*, 3 December 1984.
5. *Little Piecer No. 1.*, Halliwell Local History Society, 1987.
6. G. Readyhough, *Bolton Town Centre: A Modern History*, Richardson, no date, pp. 39–41.
7. J.H. Longworth, *The Cotton Mills of Bolton, 1780–1985*, Bolton Museum, 1987, p. 15.
8. A.D. George, 'Industrial Archaeology in Bolton and District', *Industrial Archaeology*, Vol. 11, No. 4, Spring 1977, p. 18.
9. H.C. Casserley, *British Steam Locomotives*, Bloomsbury, 1992, pp. 74–5. A model of the locomotive is also in Bolton Museum.
10. The narrow-gauge yard engine, *Wren*, is also preserved in York Railway Museum.
11. Anon., *Fifty Facts about Horwich*, leaflet published by Bolton Metropolitan Borough, no date.

CHAPTER 11

1. Men working at Walker's lime pits are featured in the video 'Bygone Bolton', by Bygone Films, BF156, 1997.
2. A very good account of Farnworth's chemical industry appears in Alan Wolstenholme's *Industrial History of Farnworth and District*, published by the author, 2000, pp. 92–107.

3. Anon., *Exploring the Croal Valley: 1*, published by Croal–Irwell Valley Warden Service, *c*. 1984, pp. 7–9.

4. B. Connor, *Little Lever*, Richardson, 1955, pp. 11, 18, 29; and *Bolton Evening News*, 28 July 1948.

5. Anon., *150 Facts about Bolton*, published by the Bolton Metropolitan Borough, 1988, Fact No. 146. A beer shop was a house above a certain rateable value, licensed under the Beerhouse Act of 1830 to sell beer but not spirits.

6. A 'hush' shop was a building where beer was brewed illegally – i.e. without a licence. They were usually in remote places, such as outlying farms, to avoid detection by the Excise men.

7. Anon., *150 Facts about Bolton*, Fact No. 10.

8. G. Readyhough, *Bolton Town Centre: A Modern History – Bradshawgate area 1900–1984*, Richardson, 1984, p. 11.

9. *Bolton a Century Ago*, Landy Publishing, 1991, p. 11.

10. 'How Roberts Transformed an Industry', *Bolton Evening News*, 28 November 1990.

CHAPTER 12

1. D. Lyddon and P. Marshall, *Paper Making in Bolton*, published by John Sherratt for Trinity Paper Mills Ltd, 1975, p. 51.

2. *Ibid.*, p. 23.

3. *Ibid.*, p. 37.

4. A walk mill, or waulk mill, is the old name for a fulling mill, in which woollen cloth was thickened. In earlier times this was done by walking or trampling the cloth under bare feet, in a similar way to treading grapes.

5. Lyddon and Marshall, *Paper Making in Bolton*, p. 106.

6. In *Paper Making in Bolton*, Lyddon and Marshall suggest the name Creams comes from the technical description of certain types of white watermarked paper, such as cream-laid and cream-wove.

7. Lyddon and Marshall, *Paper Making in Bolton*, p. 25.

8. *Ibid.*, pp. 29–30.

CHAPTER 13

1. 'Canale' is an old spelling of cannel, a type of coal found in the Wigan and Westhoughton coalfields, which burns with a clear, bright flame. It was once also called candle coal. 'Se cole' means sea coal. This name was used in London in the sixteenth century for ordinary coal brought to the city from Tyneside by ship along the east coast.

2. Quoted in D.R. Mills, *A Short History of Hall i' th' Wood*, published by the author, 1992, p. 9.

3. D. Defoe, *A Tour through England and Wales*, reprint of 1724–6 edition by Dent, 2 vols, 1928, Vol. 2, p. 266.

4. G.J. Atkinson, *The Canal Duke's Collieries*, Richardson, no date, p. 6.

5. *Ibid.*

6. The first locomotives ran on coke for many years. Coal burning was not permitted until the 1860s, after it was discovered that inserting a brick arch and deflector plate in the firebox reduced smoke emission to an acceptable level.

7. Lane, J. and Anderson, D., *Mines and Miners of South Lancashire, 1870–1950*, private pub., *c.* 1981, p. 68.

8. R. Challinor, *The Lancashire and Cheshire Miners*, Graham, 1972, pp. 25–8.

9. *Ibid.*

10. Anon., *Coal in Bolton*, Bolton Environmental Education Project, no date, p. 26.

CHAPTER 14

1. D. Rasbotham, *History of Lancashire*, 1780, quoted by D. Billington in *Little Piecer, Newsletter of the Halliwell Local History Society*, No. 26, 1989.

2. J. Kerr, 'On the Remains of Some Old Bloomeries Formerly Existing in Lancashire', *Transactions of the Historic Society of Lancashire and Cheshire*, Vol. 12 (1871–2), pp. 107–12.

3. Shingling meant hammering a white-hot lump of wrought iron just brought from a puddling furnace to force out entrained slag, turning the mass into a bloom.

4. K. Hudson, *Exploring our Industrial Past*, Hodder & Stoughton, p. 47.

5. *Bolton Evening News*, 26 April 1994.

6. *Ibid.*

7. Rivington Interpretation Team, *A Guide to Lead Mines Clough*, leaflet published by Greater Manchester and Lancashire County Councils and North West Water Authority, 1984.

8. P. Hesketh, *Rivington, Village of the Mountain Ash*, Carnegie, 1990, pp. 43–5.

CHAPTER 15

1. R. Boyson, *The Ashworth Cotton Enterprise*, Clarendon Press, 1970, p. 116.

2. *Ibid.*, p. 118

3. W. Dodd, *The Factory System Illustrated*, 1842, p. 89, quoted in Boyson, *The Ashworth Cotton Enterprise*, p. 119.

4. Boyson, *The Ashworth Cotton Enterprise*, p. 116.

5. I. Short, *The Ridgways of Horwich*, Horwich Heritage, *c.* 1933, p. 6.

6. W.D. Billington, *Barrow Bridge*, Halliwell Local History Society, 1988, pp. 14–17.

7. D. O'Connor, *Barrow Bridge, Bolton, Dean Mills Estate*, Bolton Industrial History Society, 1972, p. 25.

8. Allen Clarke ('Teddy Ashton') wrote *Tales of a Deserted Village* as a newspaper serial in 1900–1, which created much local interest in the village.

9. A.B. Reach, *Manchester and the Textile Districts in 1849*, Helmshore Local History Society, 1972, p. 67.

10. A. Clarke, *The Effects of the Factory System*, Richards, 1899, reprinted 1986 by Kelsall, pp. 133–4.

11. C.H. Saxelby, ed., *Bolton Survey*, R.S. Publishers, 1971, p. 102.

CHAPTER 16

1. W.D. Billington, *From Affetside to Yarrow*, Ross Anderson, 1982, p. 77.

2. *Ibid.*, p. 79.

3. J.J. Francis, *Affetside: An Historical Survey*, Turton Local History Society, 1996, p. 20.

4. J. Copeland, *Roads and Their Traffic, 1750–1850*, David & Charles, 1968, p. 193.

5. W.D. Billington, *Nightingales to Bolton Turnpike Trust 1763–1877*, manuscript, no date, map 8.

6. J. Clegg, *Annals of Bolton*, Bolton Chronicle, 1888, p. 64.

7. Billington, *Nightingales to Bolton Turnpike Trust*, p. 109.

8. *Little Piecer, Newsletter of the Halliwell Local History Society*, No. 20, *c.* 1988.

CHAPTER 17

1. J. Clegg, *Annals of Bolton*, Bolton Chronicle, 1888, p. 76.

2. *Bolton Chronicle*, 29 October 1829.

3. D.J. Billington, 'Nightingales to Bolton Turnpike Trust, 1763–1877', manuscript, no date, p. 52.

4. J.C. Gillham, 'A History of Bolton Corporation Transport', bound typescript, 1950, p. 1.

5. *Ibid.*, p. 2.

6. *Ibid.*, p. 7.

7. D. O'Connor, *The Motor Vehicle and Bolton: A Brief Account*, Bolton Hospice Appeal, March 1999, p. 2.

8. B. Champness, 'Merrall Brown 1919', manuscript, no date.

9. D. O'Connor, *The Motor Vehicle and Bolton*, p. 2.

CHAPTER 18

1. V.I. Tomlinson, 'The Manchester, Bolton & Bury Canal Navigation', *Transactions of the Lancashire and Cheshire Antiquarian Society*, Vols 75, 76, 1965–6, pp. 249–50.

2. *Ibid.*, p. 246.

3. *Ibid.*, p. 288.

4. Matthew Fletcher, a mining engineer and coal owner, was also a promoter of the Manchester, Bolton & Bury Canal. He surveyed the route and served on its committee. He also assisted John Nightingale, the second canal engineer, who was his nephew.

5. A.C. Banks and R.B. Schofield, *Brindley at Wet Earth Colliery*, David & Charles, 1968, p. 19.

6. *Ibid.*, p. 118.

CHAPTER 19

1. George Stephenson's estimate for the cost of the line was £49,343 1s 0d, quoted in B.T. Barton, *Historical Gleanings* (first series), Bolton Chronicle, 1881, pp. 51–2.

2. W.O. Skeat, *George Stephenson: The Engineer and His Letters*, Institution of Mechanical Engineers, 1973, pp. 77, 107. Robert, George's brother, later became chief engineer of Pendleton Collieries.

3. J. Clegg, *Annals of Bolton*, Bolton Chronicle, 1888, p. 120

4. Barton, *Historical Gleanings*, p. 361.

5. Anon., *Bolton's Disused Railways*, Bolton Environmental Education Project, no date.

6. *Ibid.*

7. *Ibid.*, p.3

8. *Ibid.*

9. H. Tompson and C. Stockton, 'Smithills Dean Tramroad', *Little Piecer, Newsletter of the Halliwell Local History Society*, No. 2, *c*. 1995.

10. J. Garrity, 'John Crankshaw's Pipeworks', private unpublished manuscript, no date.

11. Anon., *Bolton's Disused Railways*.

CHAPTER 20

1. W.E. Brown, *Robert Heywood of Bolton, 1786–1869*, S.R. Publishers, 1970, pp. 21, 47.

2. Riperian right is the ancient right of users to extract water from a river or stream. If their source of water is disturbed, compensation water has to be supplied from another source. Thus the Wayoh is a compensation reservoir for the Bradshaw Brook.

3. Brown, *Robert Heywood of Bolton*, p. 47.

4. J. Rawlinson, *About Rivington*, Nelson Bros., 1976, p. 108.

5. J. Clegg, *Chronological History of Bolton and District*, Bolton Chronicle, 1888, p. 73.

6. B.T. Barton, 'Historical Gleanings of Bolton and District', *Bolton Chronicle*, first series, 1881, p. 61.

7. *Ibid.*, pp. 67–8

8. Anon., *150 Facts about Bolton*, leaflet published by Bolton Metropolitan Borough, 1988, Fact 83.

9. P. Dunsheath, *A History of Electrical Engineering*, Faber & Faber, 1969, p. 196.

10. *Bolton Evening News*, 16 June 1995.

CHAPTER 21

1. Dates for the year(s) of office for this and subsequent paragraphs are taken from the list of mayors in *Bolton: The Golden Years, 1860–1914*, Bolton Environmental Education Project.

2. J.H. Longworth, *The Cotton Mills of Bolton, 1780–1985*, Bolton Museum, 1987, p. 106.

3. M. Harrison, *Bolton's Royal Infirmary*, Bolton General Hospital, *c*. 1997, p. 4.

4. *Ibid.*, p. 4.

FURTHER READING

CHAPTER 1

Grayson, R.F. and Williamson, I.A. (eds), *Geological Routes around Wigan*, Wigan & District Geological Society, 1977 (This has some information on the area north-west of Bolton)

CHAPTER 4

Anon., 'The Cost of Building Lancashire Loomhouses and Weavers' Workshops: the Account Book of James Brandwood of Turton, 1794–1814', *Textile History*, vol. 8, pp. 56–76

Atkinson, F., 'Water-shot Stonework', *Transactions of the Lancashire and Cheshire Antiquitarian Society*, vol. 69 (1959), pp. 141–3

Bythell, D., *The Handloom Weavers*, Cambridge University Press, 1969

Timmins, J.G., 'Handloom Weavers Cottages in Central Lancashire', U*niversity of Lancashire Occasional Paper*, no. 3, 1977

——, 'Housing Quality in Rural Textile Colonies, *c*. 1800–*c*. 1850', *Industrial Archaeological Review*, vol. xii, no. 1, May 2000

CHAPTER 5

Anon., *Concerning Cotton – A Brief Account of the Amalgamated Cotton Mills Trust Ltd*, ACMT, 1920

Armstrong, L., *Sunnyside Mills, Bolton*, Bolton Library, 1977

Bradley, J.F., 'The Evolution of the Cotton Mill in Bolton', unpublished Manchester University thesis, 1955

Catling H., *The Spinning Mule*, Lancashire Library, 1986

Holden, R.N., 'Mill Architects', *Manchester Regional Industrial Archaeological Society Newsletter*, no. 83, May 1998, pp. 6–8

Longworth J.H., *The Cotton Mills of Bolton, 1780–1985*, Bolton Museum & Art Gallery, 1986

O'Connor, D., *Barrow Bridge, Bolton, Dean Mills Estate. A Victorian Model Achievement*, Bolton Industrial History Society, 1972

Williams, M. and Farnie, D.D., *Cotton Mills in Greater Manchester*, Carnegie, 1992 (several references are made to Bolton mills)

CHAPTER 6

Longworth, J.H., *The Cotton Mills of Bolton 1780–1985*, Bolton Museum & Art Gallery 1986

Williams, M. and Farnie, D.A., *Cotton Mills in Greater Manchester*, Carnegie, 1992

CHAPTER 7

Francis, J.J., *Bradshaw Works*, Turton Local History Society, 1979

——, *Horrobin Mill, Bleachworks in the Jumbles*, Turton Local History Society, 1992

Higgins, S.H., *A History of Bleaching*, Longmans Green, 1924

Horridge, J.F., *Harwood Vale*, Turton Local History Society, 1997

Jones, B., *The Ainsworth Family of Smithills Hall, Bleachers from the 18th to the 20th Century*, Friends of Smithills Hall, 1993

Lindop, R., *History of Turton Mill*, Turton Local History Society, 1989

Longworth, J.H., *The Cotton Mills of Bolton 1780–1985*, Bolton Museum, 1987, ch. 6 and pp. 180–3

Musson, A.E. and Robinson, E., *Science and Technology in the Industrial Revolution*, Manchester University Press, 1969, ch. 8, pp. 251–337

Short, I., *The Ridgways of Horwich*, Horwich Heritage, 1993

Sykes, Sir A.J., *Concerning the Bleaching Industry*, The Bleachers Association, 1925

Woods, B., 'Mathieu Vallet – Chemist and Balloonist', *Manchester Region Industrial Archaeology Society Newsletter*, no. 87, May 1999, pp. 5–7

CHAPTER 8

Banks, A.G. and Schofield, R.B., *Brindley at Wet Earth Colliery: An Engineering Study*, David & Charles, 1968

Lindop, R., *The History of Turton Mill*, Turton Local History Society, 1989

Preece, G., *Exploring Wet Earth Colliery* (trail guide), Croal-Irwell Valley Warden Service (no date)

CHAPTER 9

Anon., *Guide to the Bolton Steam Museum, Atlas Mills*, NMES, *c.* 1991

Anon., *Mill Engine Preservation – 20 Years Work by the Northern Mill Engine Society*, NMES, 1986

Buchanan, R.A. and Watkins, G., *The Industrial Archaeology of the Stationary Steam Engine*, Allen Lane, 1976

Hayes, G., *Stationary Steam Engines*, Shire, 1979

The Flywheel, Journal of the Northern Mill Engine Society

Watkins, G., *The Stationary Steam Engine*, David & Charles, 1968

——, *The Textile Mill Engine* (2 vols), David & Charles, 1970

CHAPTER 10

Anon., *A History of Dobson & Barlow*, Dobson & Barlow, 1927

Anon. (with intro. by P. Dale), *Bolton a Century Ago*, Landy, 1991 (repr. of Historical Publishing Co. edn of 1889, which gives accounts of many industrial and commercial firms)

Anon., *Chronology & Notes of Horwich Railway Mechanics' Institute and Horwich College*, Horwich Heritage (no date)

Anon., *Horwich Works* (tour guide leaflet), British Rail Engineering (no date)

Anon., *100 Years of Engineering Progress 1833–1933 at Soho Ironworks, Bolton*, Hick Hargreaves, 1933

Aspinall, J.A.F., 'The Horwich Locomotive Works of the Lancashire & Yorkshire Railway', *Proceedings of the Institute of Civil Engineers*, vol. cxxxix, iii, 1896–7

Green, D.A., *Horwich and the Locomotive Works of the Lancashire & Yorkshire Railway Company, 1884 to 1914*, Horwich Heritage (no date)

Smith, D.M., *Horwich Locomotive Works*, Wyre, 1996

CHAPTER 11

Anon. (with intro. by P. Dale), *Bolton a Century Ago*, Landy Publishing, 1991 (repr. of Historical Publishing Co. edn of 1889, with additions)

Anon., *Exploring the Croal Valley – 1*, Croal/Irwell Valley Warden Service, c. 1984

Billington, D., 'Halliwell Brickmakers', from *Little Piecer*, Newsletter of Halliwell Local History Society, 6/7, 1986

Connor, B., *Little Lever*, Richardson, 1955

Shaw, P. and Halton, W., 'Nob End, Bolton', *British Wildlife* 10, 1998, pp. 13–17

Wostenholme, A., *Industrial History of Farnworth*, private pub., 2000

CHAPTER 12

Hampson, C.G., *150th Anniversary of Robert Fletcher & Son Ltd*, Robert Fletcher & Sons Ltd, 1973

——, *Paper Making in the Bolton and Bury District*, Robert Fletcher & Sons Ltd, 1976

Lyddon, D. and Marshall, P., *Paper in Bolton*, pub. by Sherratt for Trinity Paper Mills Ltd, 1975

Rock Hall Information Centre, Farnworth, has much information on papermaking in the immediate area, on display and in leaflets

Sharpe France, R. 'Early Paper Mills in Lancashire', *Paper Making & Paper Selling*, vol. 66, 1943

The Archer, quarterly house journal of R. Fletcher Ltd, 1954–7, copies in Farnworth Library

CHAPTER 13

Anon., *Coal in Bolton*, Bolton Environmental Project (no date)

Atkinson, G., *The Canal Duke's Collieries, Worsley, 1760–1900*, Richardson (no date)

Davies, L.T., *Collieries in Westhoughton*, unpublished manuscript, 1983

Driver, C., *Westhoughton Coal Industry, 1550–1936*, unpublished manuscript (no date)

Francis, J.J., *Bradshaw and Harwood Collieries*, Turton Local History Society, 1982

Lane, J. & Anderson, D., *Mines and Miners of South Lancaire, 1870 to 1950*, private pub., c. 1981

Morey, Margaret A., 'Pretoria Pit Disaster', bound typescript, 1978

Redmayne, Sir R.A.S., Chief Inspector of Mines, 'Verbatim Typed Transcription of Inquiry into the Pretoria Pit Disaster', 1911 (TS in Westhoughton Library)

Wood, K., *Rich Seams*, Manchester Geological and Mining Society, 1987

CHAPTER 14

Brough, J., *Wrought Iron: The End of an Era at Atlas Forge, Bolton*, Bolton Metropolitan Borough Arts Dept., 1981

Ireland, R.J., *Lead Mining on Anglezarke* (no date)

Loch, C.W., 'Forgotten Mines in Lancashire', *Mining Magazine*, vol. 74, 1946, pp. 290–4

Rivington Interpretation Team, *A Guide to Lead Mines Clough* (leaflet), Greater Manchester County Councils and North West Water Authority, 1984

Shaw, R.C., *Records of a Lancashire Family from the 12th to the 20th Centuries*, Guardian Press, 1940

Watt, J. Jnr, 'Some Account of a Mine in which the Aerated Barytes (i.e., Witherite) is Found', *Manchester Literary & Philosophical Society*, vol. 3, 1790, pp. 598ff

Williamson, I.A., 'The Anglezarke Lead Mines', *Mining Magazine*, vol. 108, 1963, pp. 133–9

CHAPTER 15

Boyson, R., *The Ashworth Cotton Enterprise*, Clarendon Press, 1970

Buxton, A.J., 'Nineteenth-century Landscapes of Bolton', dissertation University of Durham (no date)

O'Connor, D., *A Bolton Mill Village: The Eagley Story*, Neil Richardson, 2000

CHAPTER 16

Billington, W.D., 'Nightingales to Bolton Turnpike Trust 1763–1877', bound manuscript (no date)

Tupling, G.H., 'Turnpike Trusts in Lancashire', *Manchester Literary & Philosophical Society*, vol. 94, (1952/3), pp. 1–23

Woods, R., 'Westhoughton Turnpike Trust', bound typescript (no date)

CHAPTER 17

Anon., *Bolton's Last Tram: A Pictorial History*, Bolton 66 Tramcar Trust (no date)

Gillham, J.C., 'A History of Bolton Corporation Transport', bound typescript, 1950

Horsley, R., *History of the Bolton Tramways*, private pub., 1996

O'Connor, D., 'Rise and Fall of Horse Transport', article in *Bolton Evening News*, 22 July 1997

Readyhough, G., *Bolton Town Centre: A Modern History, Deansgate, Churchgate, etc., 1900–1982*, Richardson (no date) (p. 27 has a plan showing the tramway routes)

CHAPTER 18

Askam, S., *Canal-side Ramble*, Countryside Commission (series of five leaflets describing circular walks on the M. B. & B. Canal) (no date)

Owen, D., *Canals to Manchester*, Manchester University Press, ch. 5, pp. 51–62

Parker, S. and Chester-Brown, R., *A Towpath Guide*, Manchester, Bolton & Bury Canal Society, 1989

Quarterly newsletter of the Manchester, Bolton & Bury Canal Society

Shaw, P. and Halton, W., 'Nob End, Bolton', *British Wildlife*, 10, 1998, pp. 13–17

Tomlinson, V.I., 'The Manchester, Bolton and Bury Canal Navigation', *Trans. Lancashire & Cheshire Antiquarian Society*, vols 75 & 76, 1965–6, & repr. with additions by the Manchester, Bolton & Bury Canal Society

Waterson, A., *On the Manchester, Bolton & Bury Canal*, Richardson, 1985

CHAPTER 19

Anon., *Bolton's Disused Railways*, Bolton Environmental Education Project (no date)

Anon., *A History of Trinity Street Station*, Bolton Environmental Education Project (no date)

Bardsley, J.R. *The Railways of Bolton, 1824–1959*, private pub., 1960

Basnett, Lois, 'The Bolton & Leigh Railway', *Transactions of the Lancashire & Cheshire Antiquarian Society*, vol. 62, 1950–1

Marshall, J., *The Lancashire and Yorkshire Railway*, 3 vols, David & Charles, 1969–72

Simpson, B., *Railways in and around Bolton*, Foxline, 1991

Stretton, C.E., *The History of the Bolton and Leigh and Kenyon and Leigh Junction Railways*, 1901

Townley, C.H.A., *Industrial Railways of Bolton, Bury and the Manchester Coalfields*, Runpast, 1994

CHAPTER 20

Anon., *The Rivington Reservoirs* (leaflet), Greater Manchester and Lancashire County Councils and North West Water Authority, 1983

Anon., 'Water Great Achievement – Thirlmere to Manchester Pipeline Celebrates the Centenary', *Bolton Evening News*, 30 September 1994

Hoyle, M., *History of Reservoirs from Rivington to Rossendale*, North West Water, *c.* 1988

Sale, W.E. *Forerunners of the NW Electricity Board*, NW Electricity Board, 1965

Warburton, R., 'Electricity Generation in Bolton', typescript in Bolton Archives (no date)

Williams, T.I., *History of the British Gas Industry*, Oxford University Press, 1981

Wolstenholme, A., *The Industrial History of Farnworth and District, Public Utilities*, private pub., 2000, pp. 118–21

CHAPTER 21

Anon., *Lord Leverhulme and Rivington* (leaflet), Greater Manchester and Liverpool County Councils and North West Water Authority, 1983

Anon., *Souvenir of Farnworth Park Jubilee, 1864–1914*, Farnworth UDC, 1914

Brown, W.E., *Robert Heywood of Bolton 1786–1868*, SR Publishers, 1970

Jones, B., *The Ainsworth Family of Smithills Hall*, Friends of Smithills Hall, 1993

Short, I., *Ridgways of Horwich*, Horwich Heritage Local History Society (no date)

Southern, C., 'Hall History', a short note on the various residents of Mere Hall in 'The Changing Face of Bolton', *Bolton Evening News*, 6 April 1983

INDEX

Entries in *bold* refer to illustrations.